AND A NIGHTINGALE SANG ...

W9-AEJ-449

'It's a pleasure to welcome a comedy to the West End that doesn't consist of a number of middle-class citizens standing around trying to sort out their sexual and social problems over cocktails in Hampstead. C.P. Taylor's *And A Nightingale Sang* ... is a refreshingly different in its portrait of a working-class family living in Newcastle-upon-Tyne in World War Two ... The play is an unmitigated pleasure.'

Daily Express

'Every once in a while the theatre produces an evening so unexpected, so instantly recognisable as the stuff of humanity, that it rocks you back in your seat ... It is not that the characters are so remarkable. But, by showing us their comic, obsessive preoccupation with their own individual spot on God's Little Acre, C.P. Taylor manages to warm our hearts and perhaps let us in on the real secret of the human race's survival.'

Daily Mail

'The characterisation is affectionate yet sly, sceptical; the north-eastern argot has been scrupulously recorded and lovingly stitched together ... to leave a sum impression subtler than caricature, solider than whimsy, and altogether more truthful than a bald paraphrase of the story would lead anyone to suspect.'

New Statesman

Cecil P. Taylor

AND A NIGHTINGALE SANG ...

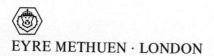

EYRE METHUEN · LONDON

First published in 1979 by Eyre Methuen Ltd
11 New Fetter Lane, London EC4P 4EE
Copyright © 1979 by Cecil P. Taylor
IBM set in 10 point Journal by 🅰 Tek-Art, Croydon, Surrey
Printed in Great Britain by Whitstable Litho Ltd
Whitstable, Kent

ISBN 0 413 46860 7

To my mother, with love

And A Nightingale Sang . . . was first staged on 10 March 1977 by Live Theatre in Newcastle-on-Tyne in a production directed by Paul Chamberlain.

And A Nightingale Sang . . . was subsequently presented by SRO Productions Limited in the version printed here at the Queen's Theatre, London on 11 July 1979, with the following cast:

HELEN STOTT, *early thirties*	Gemma Jones
JOYCE STOTT, 22, *her sister*	Veronica Sowerby
GEORGE, *fifties, her father*	Arthur Blake
PEGGY (MAM), *fifties, her mother*	Patricia Routledge
ANDIE, *seventy-odd, her grandfather*	Roger Avon
ERIC, *early twenties, Joyce's husband*	Christian Rodska
NORMAN, *early thirties*	Ray Brooks

Directed by Mike Ockrent
Designed by Geoffrey Scott
Lighting by Leonard Tucker
Incidental Music & Supervision Peter Skellern

The action of the play takes place in Newcastle-on-Tyne, during the years of World War Two.

Act One

Scene One

Oh, Johnnie, How You Can Love
Sunday, 3 September 1939

HELEN. That Sunday . . we were too busy to notice the war . . So many things were happening to us . . . The Coalman, me Da, was playing 'Oh, Johnnie' . . . . That was me Mam . . She gave everybody nicknames . . . I was 'The Cripple' . . . Me Granda was 'The Old Soldier' . . . Our Joyce was 'The Babe in the Wood' . . . We called our Mam back 'The Saint' . . . .

GEORGE. *(singing at the piano)*.
    Oh, Johnnie,
    Oh, Johnnie,
    How you can love, etc.

HELEN. Me Mam was making Sunday dinner . . . Joyce was making up her mind to say 'yes' or 'no' to Eric . . . And Granda was getting ready for Jackie's funeral . . .

ANDIE. *(with a sack)*. You want to see him before we go?

JOYCE. Ee . . . . You haven't brought him in here, Granda . . .

ANDIE. *(looking in the sack)*. He looks lovely . . . Peaceful and serene . . .

HELEN. He didn't suffer . . . You can see that . . .

ANDIE. Want to look at him George . . .

GEORGE. What do I want to see a bloody dead dog for, man . . . Get him out.

MAM. Ee . . . You haven't brought him in here . . . Put him in the bin, man . . . I've put everything in the oven . . Ready . . . . Helen . . . Are you listening to us?

GEORGE. Where you going *now*, man . . . It's near dinner time . . .

JOYCE. She's going to the chapel . . . .

GEORGE. She's just bloody *come* from the chapel . . .

ANDIE. He was a trier . . . . That was one thing about him . . wasn't it . . . *(Into the sack.)* Ee . . You were a trier son . .

GEORGE. Never even got a place . . Five years you raced him.

ANDIE. He raced his heart out; Didn't he Helen . . .

MAM. Right . . I'll be back as soon as I can . . .

GEORGE. Where are you going, man?

MAM. Father Monaghan's very upset . . . I told you . . You never listen to people . . If you'd stop banging away at that bloody piano . . .

GEORGE. I'm trying to get a chord right . . . Does that sound right . .

MAM. Father Ryan said to us . . This morning . . Coming out from Mass . . I've told you all this before . .

ANDIE. *Monaghan's* the one that let me down . . . I didn't ask him to come to the ceremony . . . I wouldn't do that . .

GEORGE. What's he rambling on about, now . . .

ANDIE. I'm talking about the funeral . . . You going to get your coat on Helen . .

HELEN. I'm coming, Grandad . . .

JOYCE. Mam . . I still don't know what I should do . . . He's coming for his dinner . . .

MAM. Give him his dinner . . .

ANDIE. I asked Monaghan . . . I've had a bereavement . .

MAM. Where's me bag?

HELEN. Mam, shouldn't you stay here . . . I know Father Monaghan's bad . . . but Eric's coming . . . and we've had the upset with Jackie . . .

MAM. You don't know what's been happening up there . . . Father Monaghan could be losing God and Christ . . Do you know that?

GEORGE. Tell him to put an advert in the Chronicle.

JOYCE. I feel rotten . . Mam . . You know . . Eric going away . . . .

MAM. I can smell that bloody animal . . . . Will you get him *out* of here!

ANDIE. He's only dead a day, man . . There's no smell from him . .

MAM. *(with disinfectant)*. Put some of that in the bag . . will you . .

JOYCE. Ee . . I couldn't go near it . . Mam . . .

MAM. *I'll* do it . .

JOYCE. Mam . . . Mam.

ANDIE. What are you doing, man . . . Putting chemicals all over the body . . .

MAM. Get it out, then . . . .

ANDIE. I'm waiting for Helen to get ready . . .

JOYCE. He's bought a ring for us and everything . . . .

MAM. I like him. He's a canny lad . . .

JOYCE. What do *you* think, Dad . . .

GEORGE. I'm just curious . . . I'd like to know . . What does she do there with all them priests . . .

JOYCE. He could be going to his

MAM. If you're interested . . They think he's had a bit of a breakdown . . . Father Monaghan . . .

JOYCE. Mam . . I want to talk to you . . Helen . . Tell us. What do you think I should do . . .

HELEN. *(to* AUDIENCE*)*. I'd been bloody telling her for the last six weeks . . . . Up every night till four o'clock in the morning telling her . . . .

ANDIE. I'm finished with the Catholic Church . . . They've let me down for the last time . . I go to Monaghan . . And say to him . . 'I don't expect you to go to me dog's funeral . .'

MAM. You didn't ask him to bury that mongrel of yours . . .

GEORGE. It's a whippet . . Bitch . . .

ANDIE. . . . . All I want is a few words . . . From the Missall . . To say over the poor soul . . .

MAM. Dogs haven't *got* a soul . . .

ANDIE. You should've heard the mouth that papist parasite opened to us . . .

JOYCE. Mam . . He's bringing the ring . . This morning . .

MAM. Do you not love him? . .

HELEN. She doesn't *know* . . .

JOYCE. I'm frightened . . Mam . . I don't know . . .

MAM. Eee . . I don't know *what* you should do, pet . . I've got to go . . .
He's always liked us . . . There's a bond between us . . . Father
Monaghan and me . . . From the first day he came here . . .

ANDIE. Are *you* coming, Joyce? . . .

MAM. How can she come . . She's waiting for her lad, man . .

ANDIE. It's a poor turn out . . Isn't it . . Two for a funeral . . . After all
that Dog's meant in the house . . Been like a baby . . .

MAM. . . . You see he's been praying for six months and fasting . . .

ANDIE. The last time . . Before we go . . Who wants to bid a last
farewell to Jackie . .

GEORGE. *Goodbye Jackie* . .

ANDIE. *(looking in the sack).* . . Gives your heart a turn, doesn't it,
Helen . . Looking at him lying there . . He's his eyes open . . He's
had a good life . . . even though he wasn't a winner . . .

MAM. After Mass . . Father Ryan came to us . . .

GEORGE. I still don't understand what she's going to do . . With
Father Monaghan . . . To keep him out of St. Nicks.

MAM. He's not going to St Nicholas . . Don't say that . . . George, man
. . . He's just having a bit of a breakdown . . .

GEORGE. Listen, if ye're going to bury the poor bugger . . Ye want te
mark the spot . . don't ye . . . Here lies Jackie . . Faithful to the
last . . Then some striking memory of him . . .

MAM. Like he was always dirtying the kitchen carpet . . .

ANDIE. You being a Catholic, should know that . . . It's a feature of
all God's creatures . . isn't it . . . They *all* shit . . . Way you can
recognise them from a stone . . . What's the difference between a
stone and a dog . . . One shits . . one doesn't . .

MAM. They don't all do their business on my kitchen carpet . . do
they . .

HELEN (*to* AUDIENCE). They were all kind of stuck there . . . The
Old Soldier with Jackie in his sack . . The Coalman . . At his

piano . . . The Saint . . with her coat on . . . The Babe in the
Wood . . . Making herself up . . just in case she was going to take
him . . . Everybody waiting for me as usual . . . to make up their
minds for them . . . I was just going to take everything in hand as
usual . . . And tell me Mam to go off to the Manse . . . And take
Grandad to Walker with the dog . . . When the doorbell rang . . .
And Joyce went white . . . Dad got up to answer it . . . Mam
stopped him . .

MAM. Wait a minute, man . . . Where you going . .

GEORGE. Going to answer the bloody door . .

JOYCE. It's *him*, Da . . . It's Eric . .

MAM. We haven't decided what's to be done . . . Have we . . .

GEORGE. Ye not think it would be easier just to say 'yes', and get
it over with . . This is bloody worse than Chamberlain running bac k
and forwards to Germany . . waiting for Hitler to make up his
mind . . *Will* I kick their teeth in . . will I not . . .

JOYCE. I don't know if I love him . .

GEORGE. I don't know if I love yer Mam . . but I'm bloody married
to her . .

MAM. Now . . That's not true . . You know that . . . That's just an
act . . . That's confusing the lass altogether.

The bell rings again.

HELEN. I'll take him in the front room . . You can't leave him at the
door . . . like that . . . till you make up your mind about taking him
or not . . .

JOYCE. Tell him I'm still getting dressed . . .

HELEN (*to* AUDIENCE). Eric was there, all his brasses shining . . .
like he'd been up all night polishing them for the great day . . And
his cap tucked in his epaulets . . .

ERIC. This is it . . . Eh, Helen . . .

HELEN. Is it? What? . . .

ERIC. Be on the wireless. Eleven o'clock . . Chamberlain . . .

HELEN. Joyce is getting dressed . . . Better come in the front room . . .
The kitchen's in a state . .

ERIC. 's alright . . Doesn't bother me . . .

HELEN. You've to come in the front room . . .

ERIC. Okey Dokey . . Front Room . . . Want to see the ring . . .

HELEN. Want a cup of tea?

ERIC. It's a nice ring . . . Got it in Glasgow . . . Going to Fort George for training . . .

HELEN. The Old Soldier's dog's dead . .

ERIC. Is he . . Shame . .

MAM. Helen . . Oh . . Hullo Eric. You're looking very smart . .

ERIC. Got the wireless on, Mrs. Stott . .?

MAM (to HELEN). Joyce wants you a minute . .
    (To ERIC.) She's just getting dressed . .

ERIC. Be on my way soon . . Mrs. Stott . . .

MAM. You not stopping for a cup of tea . .?

ERIC. I mean . . To fight old Adolf . . .

MAM. I've to go to the Church . . One of the Father's has taken bad . .

ERIC. I'm sorry about that . . Do you want to see the ring . .

HELEN. I'd better see what Joyce wants . .

MAM. I'll get you a cup of tea . . .

HELEN (to AUDIENCE). So . . . Eric was left on his own . . . Sitting in the cold sitting room . . . *Nobody* wanting to see his ring . . . Joyce . . was in the bedroom . . .

JOYCE. I don't like him . . Helen . . Do *you* like him . . I looked through the door . . at him coming in . . He smells of *bacon* doesn't he?

HELEN. Send him packing . . If you don't like him . . then . .

JOYCE. Ee . . You don't think I should do that . . . He might be going to his death . . . If I sent him away like that . . . It would be on my conscience the rest of my life . . wouldn't it . . . Just at his hour of need . . . When all I needed to say was one word . . . To make him happy . . . I kept it back . . .

HELEN. Do you *believe* that . . . Joyce . .

JOYCE. He could go away to France, happy . . .

HELEN. Joyce . . Stop it . . will you.

JOYCE. Stop what . . man . .

HELEN. Stop being in a picture . . will you . . .

JOYCE. Do you like me hair this way . . .

HELEN. Not particularly . . .

JOYCE. I'd better change it . . . Helen, what would *you* do?

HELEN (*to* AUDIENCE). What would *I* bloody do . . . I've never had
the chance . . have I? . . . With a face like mine . . and my body all
out of shape . . . If I walked down Shields Road . . naked . . no man
would look at us twice . . . I don't know what I'd do . . . I'd given up
thinking of having somebody to love us . . . I wasn't bothered . . . I
could do *without* bloody men . . Plenty other things to give you a
lift in life . . wasn't there . . . .

JOYCE. I can't even remember the colour of his eyes . . Me Mam says
they're green . . If they're green . . they're unlucky . . aren't they . . .

HELEN. Oh . . For God's sake . . Joyce . . .

JOYCE. Should I put a ribbon in my hair . . . Has he shown you the
ring . . . What it's like . .

HELEN. I haven't had time to look . . .

JOYCE. It's the idea of being tied for life to him . . .

HELEN. Not if he's going to die in France, tomorrow . . Joyce . .

JOYCE. Ee . . . Don't say that . .

HELEN (*to* AUDIENCE). And she went over to the statue of our lady
. . and bloody prayed . . .

JOYCE. . . . Dear Lady of Grace . . Please bring Eric Parker safely
through the war . . . and let him return safe and sound to his
home . . Amen . .

ANDIE. *(at the doorway with his tea).* You can forget about that . .
Joyce . . Time he'll get back from France . . he'll be an old man . .
There's his tea, Helen . . . Everything's been held up . . . I hate
being held up like this . . . I was planning the funeral for ten
o'clock . . You've to take his tea into him . . Yer Mam can't face
him just now . .

HELEN. *You* take it in . .

ANDIE. Every war . . . Gets longer and longer . . . Doesn't it . . .
The Boer War wasn't bad . . . But the 1914 war . . Four years . . .
This one . . . This one . . . I reckon . . . it should last out . . . thirty
or forty years . . . They'll stand there like two champions . .
hammering each other into the ground . .

HELEN. Take Eric's tea in . . . it's getting cold man . .

JOYCE. Ee . . Granda . . . What am I going to do . .

ANDIE. I wouldn't worry about it Joyce . . Come to the funeral with me and the Cripple . . It'll cheer you up . . .

JOYCE. One minute . . I love him . . you see, Granda . . the next I'm not sure . . .

ANDIE. It's like the tide . . you see . . . Human emotions . . They wax and wane . . . like the tide . .

JOYCE. Do they? . .

ANDIE. I don't know . . That's what it said in one of yer Mam's rubbish magazines . . . I read it last week . . . Love ebbs and flows like the tide . . . What's going to happen . . I don't want to frighten you . .

HELEN. Give us the tea . . .

ANDIE. That's right, you take it to him . . . Hitler'll bomb the whole of England . . . There'll be nowt left . . . All of England will be left in France to fight it out . . . Boom . . . Quick end . . . That's us finished . . . Best way when you think about it . . anyway . . What is living . . . Just working out some way of passing the time you're alive . . . in between eating and shitting and sleeping . . . Better to get it over in a flash like it's going to be . . isn't it . . .

HELEN. Give us that tea . .

JOYCE. Helen . . Look at his eyes . . will you . . . What colour do you think Eric's eyes are, Granda? . .

ANDIE. Yer Mam thinks it's green . .

JOYCE. Ee . . They're not . .

ANDIE. Green's her unlucky colour . . . I told her . . . If you believe it's unlucky . . It's unlucky . . . Keep off green . . . If you believe in it . . . it's true . .

HELEN (*to* AUDIENCE). I hadn't any time for the Old Soldier when he started on that analysing life thing . . . I went into Eric with his tea . . He was getting a bit impatient . . .

(*To* ERIC.) A watched kettle . . Never boils . .

ERIC. You want to see the ring . . Helen . .

HELEN. She's nearly ready . . What colour's your eyes . .

ERIC. Never looked . .

HELEN. Kind of brown . . Or could just be olive green . .

ERIC. Never thought about it . . . That's the ring . .

HELEN. It's nice . . *(Not looking at it.)* . . Your tea alright . .?

ERIC. I got it off a bloke in the pub. It's a quarter carat . . . Worth a lot of money . . Course I didn't ask him where *he* got it . . . Nice isn't it . . .

HELEN. So you're off to France . .

ERIC. Not allowed to say where we're going . . In case the Germans get to know . . Spies . . You know . . . She nearly ready . . .? I'm going to Morpeth . . . Longhorsley — near Morpeth for training.

HELEN. You're *not* going to France . .?

ERIC. Not tomorrow . . Will . . you know . . when it's time . . Where you going?

HELEN. I forgot to get you a biscuit . . *(Going to* JOYCE.) He's not going to France . . .

MAM. Thank God . . . and the Sacred Heart . . for answering me prayers . .

JOYCE. Thank you, Dear Lady . . .

HELEN. He's going to Morpeth . . .

MAM. Ee . . What a relief . . . I'd better get to the Manse then . .

JOYCE. Mam, wait a minute, man . . . What should I do? . .

HELEN. He's not going to his death for a month or so . . till he's finished his training . . .

JOYCE. Did you see the ring . . . What's it like?

HELEN. It's a half a carat diamond solitaire . . Looks nice enough . .

JOYCE. Ee . . Is it . . .

MAM. What colour's his eyes . . They're green . . aren't they . .

HELEN. Brown . . Brownish green . . Olive green . . I don't know . . Pink . . .

JOYCE. What do you think about this ribbon . .

MAM. It's nice, pet . . It's understandable . . . If a priest has prayed night and day and fasted . . . for peace . . . and then this happens . . . It's a trial to his faith . . . .

HELEN. I'd better take him in a biscuit . . and you'd better come in and talk to him right away . . . .

(*To* AUDIENCE.) In the sitting room . . The Coalman was entertaining Eric . . Now . . Playing the Last Post . . on his mouth organ . . . .

(*To* ERIC.) She's nearly ready . . . .

ERIC. Okey dokey . . . Do you want to see the ring, Mr. Stott . .

HELEN. Would it not be in your Army Card . . . Your eye colour . . .

ERIC. Would it?

GEORGE. I think for myself . . . Always have thought for myself . . . I don't let any man dictate to me what I should think . . . About Hitler or anything else . . . . I mean . . You can see Hitler's point about the Poles . . Going into Poland . . . Very dodgy people, the Poles . . . Swychinsky . . . Ted Swychinsky . . . Know him?

ERIC. I don't know him . . .

HELEN. Let's see your card, Eric . .

GEORGE. He stole my horse . . Put us out of business . . 1937 . . . .

ERIC. Sorry to hear that, Mr. Stott . . .

GEORGE. You had to change your horses when I was in the coal trade . . winter . . spring . . Sold the spring horse . . and bought a heavier one for winter . . other way round spring . . . I was bad with me chest . . That spring . . Swychinsky . . my mate . . Says: I'll take the horse to market . . . . £22 . . Reserve . . . I'm showing you the kind of character your Pole is . .

ERIC. Got it . . . (*with the card.*)

HELEN. Does it say . .?

ERIC. Looking . . .

GEORGE. Does a deal outside the ring . . Seventeen quid . . Pockets it . . and runs off to Middlesbrough with the seventeen quid . . drinks and whores it till its done . . . That's me out of the coal trade . . No horse . . . Finished . . That's the Poles for you . . .

ERIC. It says . . Olive Green . .

HELEN. Does it . . .

MAM. She wants you again. (*To* ERIC.) She got a stain on her dress and had to change it . .

HELEN. I'd better go to her . .

(*To* AUDIENCE.) Joyce was writing a letter . .

JOYCE. I'm writing to him, Helen . . . I'm writing him a nice letter.

HELEN. Send him a telegram, man . . It'll be quicker.. .

JOYCE. Don't start getting sarky with us, Helen . . Just now . . That'll finish us altogether . . .

MAM. Is she nearly ready . . .

HELEN. You go off to Father Monaghan . . Mam . . It's alright . .

MAM. Ee . . I *couldn't* . . And leave everything on you . .

ANDIE. Are we *going*? . .

MAM. Will you get him out of here . . Joyce is changing . . .

JOYCE. . . . . Dear Eric, It is easier to say this in a letter . . .

HELEN (*to* AUDIENCE). And at that minute, Hitler turned up . . Mam was just saying . .

MAM. What I might do is nip out for a minute . . to tell them I'll be held up going to see the Father . . What do you think Helen . . (*Sirens.*)

ANDIE. Christ! The Bloody Germans . .

HELEN (*to* AUDIENCE). Ee . . That miserable sound . . Everybody turned white . . . It had us trembling . . I don't know what it was . . It was the first time in my life . . I'd been really terrified . . .

MAM. What are we going to do Helen . . What are we going to do . . .

GEORGE. It's the bloody sirens . . . You hear them . . .

MAM. George . . What are we going to do . . .

GEORGE. What's Joyce doing . .

HELEN. She's writing a letter . . .

   (*To* AUDIENCE.) And then Eric came in . . and completely took over . .

ERIC. Get your gas masks . . Hullo Joyce . .

JOYCE. Hullo Eric . . I was just writing to you . . .

ERIC. Get your gas mask, man . . .

JOYCE. I'll get it Eric . . .

ERIC. Everybody get your gas masks . . . We've been told . . The first time they come over . . they'll probably drop gas . . to surprise us . . Better get into the kitchen . . .

HELEN (*to* AUDIENCE). He pushed us all into the kitchen . . . and started stuffing towels and that into the cracks in the door . . .

MAM. (*with her mask.*) Eric . . What are we going to do . . These things don't work . . Do they? . .

ERIC. Seal up all the doors . . .

ANDIE. I've got to get to Walker Park, Eric, man . . to bury me dog! . . .

ERIC. Put that fire out, somebody . .

MAM. What are you looking for now man . .

GEORGE. Where's last night's chronicle . . It's in the Chronicle . . . What to do in air raids . .

ERIC. I know what to do in air raids, Mr. Stott . . . Get your gas mask . . .

GEORGE. I'm checking for meself . . .

ERIC. Will you get your gas mask, Mr. Ryan . .

ANDIE. There's nothing to worry about, son . . . We are here . . by a mistake . . . An accident . . .

MAM. For God's sakes, Da . . . Don't start that, now . . (*To* ERIC.) You're putting out the fire . .

ERIC. That's right . . . Get us some blankets . .

ANDIE. If we die, we die. It's not as deadly as people think dying.

GEORGE. Where's me bloody *chronicle,* man . . .

MAM. I think I cut it up . . . It's in the netty . . . Where's he going . . . Stop him . .

GEORGE. I'm going to get me Chronic . . .

MAM. You'll get bombed, George man . . Stay where you are . . .

ERIC. The planes might take a bit to get here . . . We'll hear them . . . First thing we'll hear . . . is the Anti-Aircraft guns going off . .

JOYCE. Is that what you hear first Eric . .

ERIC. That's what you hear first . . .

GEORGE. (*returning with the Chronicle*). You're pretty sharp, aren't you . . Using me Chronicle for netty paper . . aren't you . . . I don't know *where* it is, now . . . Eric . . man . . That's a good blanket . . . Stop him man . . Stuffing a good blanket like that up the chimney . . .

ERIC. Keeping the gas out, aren't we . . .

ANDIE. I'm telling you, let it in, man . . And finish it off once and for all . . .

MAM. Ee . . Do you think poor Father Monaghan's going to survive all this, Helen? . . .

JOYCE. Will I help you, Eric . .

ANDIE. Work it out for yourselves . . People's like a disease . . on the earth . . . That's what I'm talking about . .

GEORGE. I've got it . . . This man was out in Spain . . and was in dozens of air raids . . . It says you don't need to worry about air raids . . .

ANDIE. That's what I'm talking about . . . Listen . . . You get born . . . right . . You grow up . . . You hang around . . all your life . . . Grafting your life away . . . What for? . . .

ERIC. No planes yet?

JOYCE. Are there not . .

GEORGE. *(reading).* I have been in dozens of air raids . . . People think air raids are worse than they really are . . Believe me . . If you take the proper precautions . . You can survive the worst raid . .

ANDIE. You end up losing your teeth . . your hair . . everything . . . waiting for your time to come . . . What's the point . . . Take Jackie . . . Died in his prime . . . With all his faculties . .

HELEN. Granda, Sit down, man . . . And take it easy . . .

ANDIE. I'm telling you . . . We'd be doing everybody a good turn . . . Getting the earth clean of a disease . . People . . Digging into it . . . burning it . . . Killing all the animals . . . You should've seen Flanders when we left it . . 1917 . . . .

GEORGE. When you hear the planes coming . . Throw yourself on the ground . .

ERIC. That's just when you've no cover, Mr. Stott . .

GEORGE. Are you trying to argue with a man who has been through dozens of air raids . . .

ANDIE. Not a tree left standing . . . Everything flattened . . not a bit of green . . the whole earth churned up . . . I'm telling you . . We're better out of it . . . For everybody's sake . . .

JOYCE. Ee . . I'm frightened, Eric . . .

ERIC. It's all right . . . Got everything organised . . .

JOYCE. If *you* weren't here . . Eric . .

GEORGE. We'd had Hitler jumping through the kitchen window . . . . Now . . This is important . . Listen to this . .

MAM. I wish you wouldn't read that . . It upsets us . . . Listening to things like that . . .

GEORGE. The bomb makes a rushing screaming sound as it approaches . .

MAM. I'm not listening . . . George . . .

GEORGE. As soon as you hear that . . . Get down on the ground . . Throw yourself on the ground . . .

ANDIE. When you think about it . . He's better out of it, isn't he, Helen . . Our Jackie . .

HELEN. He is Granda . .

GEORGE. Another feature of an air raid . . After the planes have dropped their bombs . . *(Breaks off.)*

JOYCE. What happens, then, Dad . . .

GEORGE. It's torn up . . . Somebody's used what happens next for wiping themselves on . . .

JOYCE. What else do they do, Eric? . .

ERIC. They machine gun you . .

MAM. Joyce, Helen — come with me . .

JOYCE. Where are you going, Mam . . .

MAM. I want you with us . . The two girls . . . Eric . . I'm sorry . . I must ask Our Lady something . . . . If I don't . . we'll never get out of here alive . .

ERIC. I've sealed up the doors, Mrs. Stott . . .

MAM. I must get to me Our Lady . . .

GEORGE. Just use your Rosary, man . . for God's sake . . .

MAM. Will you let me get to Our Lady, for God's sake . . .

HELEN. Mam . . Calm yourself . .

MAM. How can I calm meself when I can't get to Our Lady in me hour of need . . . Dear God in heaven . . . Will you let me get to Our Lady!

ERIC. I'm pulling it down, Mrs. Stott . . .

HELEN. (*to* AUDIENCE). And then . . . . It was all our nerves being strung up that did it . . . There was this whine . . . And all of us threw ourselves on the floor . . . Even Granda . . . Then I suddenly realised what the noise was . . . (*She gets up. Goes into the scullery. Returns with the kettle.*) It was the kettle, mam.

MAM. That was your fault, George . . Putting it into people's heads about air raids . . .

ERIC. Better be safe than sorry, Mrs. Stott . . .

They all get up except ANDIE.

ANDIE. Is it all right . . .

HELEN. It was the kettle, Granda . . .

ANDIE. I *thought* it was the kettle . . .

HELEN. Seeing it's boiling . . . I might as well make everybody a cup of tea . . . Will I . . .

JOYCE. You want to see me ring, everybody?

MAM. Yer ring?

HELEN. Your ring?

(*To* AUDIENCE.) God knows when she got it . . . I found out later . . when they were lying on the ground . . . She just said 'yes' to him . . . . So that was how our Joyce got engaged . . . and how Hitler changed my life too . . .

MAM. Eee . . It's a lovely ring . . Isn't it . . .

GEORGE. Cannie . .

HELEN. It's nice . .

MAM. Eee . . Look at the state of me blankets and pillows . . .

GEORGE. There's a war on, man . . . What's a bit of soot on a pillow . . .

HELEN (*to* AUDIENCE). I was watching our Joyce with Eric . . Sitting at the table . . drinking their tea . . . Joyce not being able to keep her eyes off the ring . . . . shining on her finger . . I just had to think of the song . . the Coalman was playing . . He was sitting at the piano . . with his mug of tea on the top . . . . Playing away . . . .

Oh Johnnie, Oh Johnnie,
How you can love,
Oh Johnnie, Oh Johnnie,

Heavens above,
You make my glad heart jump with joy . . . etc . . .

. . . I can just bring it right back . . the smells and the sight . . and
the sound . . and all me feelings . . watching the two of them . .
sitting there . .

Oh Johnnie . . etc . . . .

Scene Two

We'll Meet Again . . .
20, 21 June 1940

HELEN (*to* AUDIENCE). The only place he knew in Newcastle was
Eldon Square . . There was a bench, under a three . . . He said to
meet him in Eldon Square . . . on Sunday afternoon . . . I really
thought he was having us on . . I went . . I sat down on the seat . .
There was nobody there but me . . . No sign of him . . . . I felt
funny sitting there . . Waiting for him . . . . I felt funny going down
to Eldon Square . .

It was one of these bad days for my ankle . . . Some days it really
got us down . . . I walked worse than ever . . It might've been my
nerves . . . I don't know . . . I had on a swagger coat, I'd just bought
that week in Parish's . . and turban . . Cost us three and eleven . . me
turban . . I looked in the mirror before I went off . . and I looked
terrible . . . He was hours late . . . I'd brought the Sun with us . . .
Just not to look daft, sitting on me own . . I saw him coming across
the Square . . But I kidded on I was reading me Sunday Sun . . .

NORMAN. It's me . .

HELEN. Oh . . So I see . .
(*To* AUDIENCE.) They'd already given him his nickname . . He was
the Tailor's Dummy . . . He was always so neat and tidy . . and his
face was scrubbed so clean . . I was nearly saying to him: Hullo,
Tailor's dummy . . .

NORMAN. What do you fancy doing?

HELEN. *(looking at him)*. I like this square . .

NORMAN. Bought you some chocolates . .

HELEN. Where did you manage to get them . . .

NORMAN. . . . You know . . . If you look you can find . . . You mind if
I say something to you . . . Eric'll have told you . . I'm a straight
forward chap . . . I saw right away . . you were a very honest,
straightforward person yourself . .

HELEN *waits for the worst.*

   I don't think your turban does you justice . . .

HELEN. I just bought it Thursday . . In Parish's . . .

NORMAN. You don't mind me being straightforward with you . . Do
you? . .

HELEN. It doesn't matter what I wear . . . I look horrible . . Anything
I put on . . You get one of them Paris dress designers to make us an
outfit . . . and I'll still look like something out of a jumble sale . . .
It doesn't bother us . . .

NORMAN. That's not true . . I don't believe that . .

HELEN. It *doesn't* bother us . . .

NORMAN. I meant *you* looking like somebody out of a jumble sale . . .
What do you think I asked you out for . . . If I didn't think you
looked nice . . . Are you angry with me . . because I said I didn't like
your turban . . .

HELEN. I don't *think* so . .

NORMAN. Where would you like to go . . Will we go for a coffee . . . I
fancy a coffee . . .

HELEN. I'd like to go up to see the Barrage Balloons . . . In the Leazes
Park . . I like seeing them . . . I like watching them winding them up
and down . . .

NORMAN. *(looking.)* They're up just now . .

HELEN. They might come down later . . for a bit . . .

NORMAN. Yes . . We'll go and have a look at them then . .

HELEN. Sit down . . .

NORMAN. I thought we were going to see that Barrage Balloon . .

HELEN. I just want to sit here for a minute . . . I like sitting here . . .

NORMAN. Call it *our* square . . then . . will we? . . .

HELEN. 'Our'? . . . .

(*To* AUDIENCE.) See . . . I just didn't know what to say to him . . .
or how to treat him . . Or anything . . . I felt really funny . . and
awkward . . and ugly . . . and a mess . . .

NORMAN. I meant the shape of your face . . That turban . .

HELEN. If it bothers you . . I'll take it off . . .

NORMAN. Yes. Take it off . . Will you . . .

HELEN *takes off the turban.*

HELEN. Is that better? . .

NORMAN. That's smashing . . It is . . . I'm telling you . . It's got a
lovely shape . . your face . .

HELEN. That's good, then . . .

NORMAN. It has . .

HELEN. All right . . It has . . About the only thing about us that has
any shape . . .

NORMAN. That's not true . . And you know it . . .

HELEN (*to* AUDIENCE) . . . And he took me hand . . It made us
really feel funny . . I went red and everything . . . I couldn't take
it away from him . . . .

(*To him.*) Will we go up the Leazes, then . . .

NORMAN. Right . . .

HELEN (*to* AUDIENCE). He still held my hand . . . We walked
awkwardly out of the square towards the park . . I was limping
really bad . . . Saying to myself . . . That's the last time he's going to
ask us out with him . . And I'm not bothered anyway . . . . Bloody
Eric's fault . . . Bringing him back to Walker in the first place . . .
It was the Ferry week . . The Coalman was playing 'I love to ride a
ferry' all bloody week . . . . Middle of June . . I was on night shift . .
At Parsons . . . Dad was, too . . . Labouring at the Neptune Yard . . . .

GEORGE.   I love to ride a ferry,
               Where music is so merry,
               There's a man who plays the concertina,
               On a moonlit upper deck arena . . .
               Where people all are dancing,

Where couples are romancing,
Life is like a mandolin,
Life is like a mandolin,
Happy, we sing together,
Happy, we cling together,
Happy with the ferryboat serenade . . . .

HELEN (*to* AUDIENCE) . . . That first time Norman came into my life.
It was one of *those* perfect June days . . . I was sitting out on the
step, in the back yard . . . Eric had disappeared to France, after two
days honeymoon with Joyce in Walker . . . and we'd never heard
from his since . . . I could get nowt out of Joyce . . *How* she felt . .
Everybody was sure he was dead . . . The last of them had got out of
Dunkirk three weeks back . . . and *still* we hadn't heard from
Eric . . . . First thing that happened was the Old Soldier turned
up . . . Two weeks early . . from Auntie Marge's . . . With all his
luggage . . .

ANDIE. I stood out there . . Listen to us . . George . . . . I stood out
there . . *Entranced* with the music . . .

HELEN. Granda . . You're two weeks *early* . .

ANDIE. No use asking me . . if I'm two weeks early . . or two weeks
late . .

GEORGE. You're two weeks early . .

ANDIE. There's a war on . . Different routines in wartime . . . . Where's
The Saint? . .

GEORGE. I was thinking of putting a mattress in the shelter . . We've
got a shelter, now . . . Did you know? . . . . When I'm on nightshift . . .
It's the best place . . Nobody disturbs us there . . .

HELEN. Does me Mam know you're coming . . She doesn't Granda . .
Does she? . .

GEORGE. She's gone to the Chapel . . There's a new Father . . .
Monaghan's gone to be a Chaplain . . Did you hear . . .

ANDIE. I told you, Helen, man . . It's out of me hands . . . . Not for
me to reason why . . . They work it out between them . . Where me
next pillow is . . George . . You should never have daughters . . Take
your whole life over, daughters . . I know . . Ye've got them . . .
Don't say you haven't been warned . . .

GEORGE. I told her to take her statue to see the new priest . . . An
outing for her Virgin Mary . . . Give her a bit of fresh air . . .

HELEN. What did you fight with Auntie Marge over, *this* time . .

ANDIE. You should tell yer Da' . . never to laugh at what people believe in . . .

GEORGE. Ye're right, Andie . . . I shouldn't . . .

ANDIE. If they believe in it . . . It's true . . .

GEORGE. It is . . .

ANDIE. I wish *I* bloody believed in something . . .

GEORGE. I believe in Churchill . . . You liked that song . . did you? . .

ANDIE. It's a lovely song, George . . . An excellent cherry song . . excellently played . . .

HELEN. She's got it marked on the calendar . . when you're due . . Look . . . June 24th . . Father . . .

ANDIE. You know that, Helen . . I just take my orders . . They say to us: 'Time you moved on to Peggy . . . Pack yer bags . .' I pack my bags and take me cat . . and move on to Peggy . . Mine is not to reason why . .

GEORGE. Quite right. Best way . . . Move in with me in the shelter . . .

ANDIE. Have ye a pan . . I got a bit of fish for Tibbie . . .

HELEN. Granda . . You're not starting cooking stinking cat fish on top of you turning up two weeks too soon . . . You know how she hates the smell of cat fish . .

ANDIE. Look at them . . cod lugs . . Fresh out the North Sea this morning . . A penny . . .

HELEN. Granda . . Your bed's not made or anything, man . . We haven't changed round the room for you . . .

GEORGE. He's sleeping with me in the shelter . .

ANDIE. I don't think I can sleep in the shelter . .

GEORGE. Give you a hot water bottle . . . (*Mimics an air raid warning.*)

ANDIE *is intent on his cat fish.*

GEORGE. It's Peggy . . The old woman . . She's coming now . .

ANDIE. Listen . . . I think I'll lie down . . A bit . . . . Just tell her I'm here, Helen . . Say . . I was a bit tired . .

HELEN (*to* AUDIENCE). And he ran off with his case and Tibbie . . . It was his lucky day, but . . First thing me Mam did, when she came in, was go to the statue of Our Lady in her room . . .

MAM. George . . Helen . . Come and look . . .

HELEN (*to* AUDIENCE). Me Mam was standing at the statue of Our Lady . . .

MAM. Can you see? . .

GEORGE. I'm looking . . .

HELEN. What do you see, Ma . .

MAM. Can you not see yourself . . . Look at Our Lady . . .

HELEN. The sun's lovely on her . . .

MAM. She's changed her expression . .

GEORGE. I'm away back to me piano . . .

MAM. George, man . . Look at her . . .

GEORGE. (*not interested*). She's changed her expression . . .

MAM. She has. She's smiling . . . Can you not see, Helen?

HELEN. I'm not sure, Mam . . .

MAM. I felt it, at the chapel . . Helen . . . I was standing there, praying . . . for Eric . . . And I felt meself all glowing . . . And I came rushing back here . . . And Our Lady's smiling at us . . . Do you not see, Helen . . .

HELEN. Eee . . I don't know, Mam . . Maybe . .

MAM. I had this lovely warm feeling . . Kneeling there in the church . . .

HELEN (*to* AUDIENCE). Dad was at his piano, again . . Playing that Vera Lynn song . . . Granda's fish was boiling . . . for his cat . . . .

GEORGE   We'll meet again,
               Don't know where,
               Don't know when . .

MAM. What's that smell? . .

GEORGE.   But I know we'll meet again,
               Some sunny day . . .

MAM. Who's cooking fish, Helen? . .

GEORGE.   Keep smiling through. Just like you always do,
               Till the blue skies drive the dark clouds far away . .

MAM. (*at the fish*). . . Where *is* he? When did the Old Soldier come?

HELEN. He's just a few days early, Mam . . .

MAM. Da .! Da .! Where are you, man . .

GEORGE.   So will you please say hello,
            To the folks that I know,
            Tell them I won't be long,

MAM. Da!

GEORGE.   They'll be happy to know, . .

MAM. Da . . .

HELEN. It's all right . . I'll make his bed . . later . .

ANDIE. *(coming in, guilt all over his face).* What it was . . Peggy . . .

MAM. You're two weeks too early, Da, man . . It's not fair . . I'm glad
to see you . . But . . . . An agreement's an agreement . . . Margaret's
to pull her weight along with the rest of us . .

ANDIE. I'm telling you what happened . . This morning . . . . The sun
was shining . .

GEORGE.   They'll be happy to know that as you saw me go . . I was
            singing this song . .

MAM. George, can you not give that bloody piano a rest!

ANDIE. What I said to myself was . . It just came into me head,
Peggy . . Listen to this . . . . Eric is alive and safe and well . .

MAM. Ee . . It didn't, Da . . Did it? . .

ANDIE. I'm telling you . . .

HELEN (*to* AUDIENCE). Me Mam looked straight in his eyes . . . .
Reading him like a book . . .

ANDIE. All right . . . I'm telling you a lie . . . . People tell people lies . . .
man . . I made a mistake . . I thought it was time I was here . . I
packed me bags . . And everything . . this morning . . . And when I
found out I was two weeks too early . . .

The truth is . . Keep this to yerself . . Peggy . . . I can't help it . .
man . . You're me favourite daughter . . . .

MAM. Oh . . For God's sake, Da . . .

ANDIE. You are, man . . I can't help it . . It's the truth . . I miss you . .
The six months I'm at me other daughter's house . . I'm missing
you . . .

MAM. Come and see the statue of Our Lady . . Da . . .

HELEN (*to* AUDIENCE) . . . They went in to see the statue . . . . The Coalman started up again . . .

GEORGE.   We'll meet again . . Don't know where, don't know when . . . But I know we'll meet again, some sunny day . . .

ANDIE. *(coming back).* . . . Thank God, then . . He's saved . . . Joyce's man . . Eh . . .

HELEN. Granda, man . . Don't be daft, man . . You don't believe that statue's smiling . . .

ANDIE. If she says it is . . it is . . . Anyway . . It doesn't matter . . Nothing matters . . . Does it . . . We're all bits of life, dancing away, till we burn ourselves out . . .

GEORGE. Or bloody Hitler does it for us . . .

HELEN. Ee . . You're a daft old bugger . . aren't you . .
(*To* AUDIENCE.) He was at the cooker . . Stirring his cat fish . .

ANDIE. Cannie bit of cod lug that . . . She'll really enjoy that, Tibbie . . . . Smell it . . .

GEORGE. Bloody smell it alright . . . I'm thinking of putting on me bloody gas mask . . .

HELEN (*to* AUDIENCE) . . . Me Mam must have left the front door open in her excitement . . . Because the Coalman was just saying that . . . When the Lost Boy was in the room with this other soldier . . . Standing there . . . It was like a miracle . . It really was . . The way they were suddenly standing there . . .

ERIC. I'm back, then . .

GEORGE. Eric . . Come here, lad . . Give us yer hand . . . Welcome back son . .

ERIC. Where's the lass, then . . ?

HELEN. She's been very worried about you . . Why didn't you write to her . . .

ERIC. Where *is* she, Helen, man? . .

ANDIE. Who's *he*?

ERIC. Him?

NORMAN. I'm Norman . . .

ERIC. He's from Birmingham.

GEORGE. Peggy, man . . Where are you . . The lad's back . . Where are you . . .

ERIC. Just come from Durham . . .

HELEN. Why didn't you let her know you were back . . .

ERIC. I wrote a letter . . And gave it to this tart . . In Southampton . . .

MAM. Ee . . I can't believe it . . Eric, son . . ! Ee . . *Look* at you . . You're back ! . . . Helen . . Are you going to give them a cup of tea . . .

ERIC. Where's the lass? . .

HELEN. I'll go and get her . . . She's at Parsons . . . She's a job . . at the Blade shop . . I'll get her out . . .

MAM. Did you tell him about Our Lady . . .

GEORGE. We told him about Our Lady . . .

MAM. Isn't that a *miracle*, Eric . . .

ERIC. We all got this letter thing to fill in . . To the next of kin . . . I gave it to this tart . . In Southampton . .

MAM. Did you have a terrible time, pet . . . Getting clear of the Germans . . .

NORMAN. We were lucky. We found this shop with tins of beans . . .

ERIC. Eating cold beans all the way to bloody Dunkirk . . . You ever eaten cold beans . . night and day . . Geordie . . ?

MAM. I've got some sausage and dried egg . . . Would you fancy sausage and dried egg . . .

ERIC. Oh . . I brought you a present (*Handing her a packet of soap powder.*)

MAM. Oh, soap powder! That's nice of you . . .

GEORGE. I was just playing that song . . We'll meet again . . Minute you came in . .

ERIC. So you didn't get me letter? . . I gave it to a tart . . .

HELEN. I'm off to get Joyce . . .

ERIC. Tell her I've a present for her . . .

HELEN. I will . . .

GEORGE. Ye brought her soap powder, too . .

MAM. George, man . . .

ERIC. I just saw it in a shop in Durham . . Had this notice in the
   window . . Soap powder . . .

MAM. Eee . . Our Joyce's face . . Helen . . When she sees Eric . .

HELEN (*to* AUDIENCE). Our Joyce . . When I got her out of
   Parsons . . . Halfway home . . she got cold feet . .

JOYCE. What's he like, Helen? . . .

HELEN. He's waiting for you, Joyce . .

JOYCE. Helen . . I can't remember what he's like . . . His face . .

HELEN. Look at his photograph in yer bag . . .

JOYCE. I don't know what to *say* to him . . .

HELEN. Joyce, don't be daft, man . . . Come on . . .

JOYCE. Wait on, Helen . . I need a minute or two to get us together . .
   Is he wearing his uniform . . . He's not going to sleep in our house . .
   tonight . . is he? . . . What did he say? . .

HELEN. Joyce . . . Come on . . .

JOYCE. He'll want to do it with us . . tonight . . Minute we go to
   bed . . . I don't mind him . . . Going to the pictures with him . . and
   that . . But I can't stand it . . when he's all over us . .

HELEN. You'll be alright, Joyce . . When you get together . . . and see
   him . . . He's got a present for you . . .

JOYCE. What's he brought . . Stockings . . .

HELEN. Brought me Mam soap powder . . .

JOYCE. I've only known him three days . . haven't I . . . If you count it
   all up . . . You can't blame us . . . I don't know him . . . I've
   forgotten all about him . . . I know Geoff Howard in the factory ten
   times better than I know him . . .

HELEN. You'll be alright . . Once you've broken the ice again . .

JOYCE. You keep saying that . . .

HELEN. It's true . .

JOYCE. Eee . . You do some mad things in yer life, don't you? . . .
   I *married* him . . . Helen . . . Can you imagine that . . . married *him!*

HELEN. Are you coming . . Joyce, man . .

JOYCE. What am I going to say to him . . .

HELEN (*to* AUDIENCE) . . . . The Lost Boy couldn't hear *what* she said to him . . The Coalman was making such a bloody row on the piano . . .

GEORGE.   So will you please say hello,
To the folks that I know
Tell them I won't be long . .

JOYCE. Hullo, Eric . . .

ERIC. What do you say? . . .

JOYCE. Hullo . . .

ERIC. I'll come nearer . . .

MAM. George . . . Give that bloody piano a rest . . . Will you . . People want to talk . . (*To* JOYCE.) Are you not going to give him a kiss . .

JOYCE. Yes . . . *(Not kissing him.)*

ERIC. I'm back then . . I gave this letter to a tart . . Did you get it . . .

JOYCE. I didn't get anything . . No . . .

ANDIE. I'd better come back after his leave . . I came two weeks before me time, Joyce . .

ERIC. I've got three days . . .

JOYCE. It's alright . . Granda, man . . Don't move out for us . . . Eric can sleep in his Mam's . . can't you Eric . . .

ERIC. It's away over in Heaton, Joyce, man . . . You don't want us . . on me first leave, back from France, for you to sleep in Walker and me over in Heaton . .

ANDIE. Listen, it's for the war effort . . . I'll go back to yer Auntie Margaret's, Joyce . .

JOYCE. Granda . . I don't *want* you to go back . . . I like you here . . .

HELEN (*to* AUDIENCE) . . . That was news to him . . Joyce never bloody *looked* at him, whenever he was with us . . .

GEORGE. How about a double mattress in the shelter . . with a hot water bottle . . That was what I was thinking of . .

MAM. Don't be daft, George, man . . . What would they be doing in the bloody shelter . .

GEORGE. Bloody more than they'd be doing, with him in Heaton and her in Walker . .

JOYCE. Do you want a cup of tea, Eric . . .

ERIC. Yer Mam's given us one . .

JOYCE. I think *I'll* have one . .

HELEN (*to* AUDIENCE) . . . Joyce went into the scullery to make the
tea . . Eric was going to follow her . . She stopped him . .

JOYCE. You'd better stay and talk to me Mam and Da' . . Eric . .

ANDIE. Should I go then . . What do you think I should do . . .

GEORGE. You'll have that poor bloody cat dizzy . . Picking it up and
putting it down again . . .

HELEN. I'd better go to the butchers and see if I can get something for
tea, Mam . .

MAM. Ee . . You'd better . . That's right . . .

HELEN (*to* AUDIENCE). Anything to get out of that
atmosphere . . . . When I got back . . Me Granda was off with his
cases and Tibbie . . . Me Mam and Dad had gone off with Norman
to Shields Road . . . Norman wanted to buy something for his Dad's
birthday or something . . . Joyce was sitting there . . . drinking her
tea . . . She'd put on fresh make up . . . But you could see she'd
been crying . . . I felt really sorry for her . . . Me heart went right out
out to her . . . Then I said to meself . . What for . . What do you
feel sorry for her for . . . She's at least got somebody . . . Even if
Eric . . Anyway . . What's wrong with Eric . . . .

(*To* JOYCE *and* ERIC.) . . . I got some liver . . .

ERIC. Yes . . I fancy a bit of liver and onions . . .

JOYCE. That's good . . .

HELEN. I'll go and get things ready for the tea, then . . .

JOYCE. I'll help you . . .

HELEN. I don't need any help . . I can peel onions and potatoes
without you helping me . . . Sit down and finish your tea . . . .

(*To* AUDIENCE.) I shut meself up in the scullery . . . . From time
to time I heard bits of the talk . .

ERIC. Going to give us a kiss . .

JOYCE. Ahuh . .

ERIC. Go on, then . .

JOYCE. (*a peck*). There you are . .

ERIC. That's not a kiss . .

JOYCE. What is it, then . . If it isn't . . .

ERIC. That's a kiss . . .

JOYCE. Ee . . Stop . . Man . . I can't breathe . . .

ERIC. That's more like it, isn't it . . . Did you miss us . . .

JOYCE. Ahuh.

ERIC. I missed you . . I thought about you all the time . .

JOYCE. That's good . . .

ERIC. I bought you a present . . .

JOYCE. Ta . .

ERIC. Want to see it . . .

JOYCE. Ahuh . .

ERIC. Give us a kiss and I'll show you it . .

JOYCE. *Don't* man — somebody'll come in . .

ERIC. It's only Helen in there . . *She's* not bothered . . . Come on . . .

JOYCE. You've been to the pub . . .

ERIC. Just for a couple . . . There you are . . What do you think . .
    (Holding up a pair of French knickers.)

JOYCE. Where did you get *them* from . . .

ERIC. Tart gave us them out of gratitude. . No she didn't . . Bought
    them . . in France . . Real French Knickers . . .

JOYCE. Ee . . I couldn't wear *them* . . !

ERIC. Of course you could . . I've been thinking about you in them,
    ever since I got them . . . .

JOYCE. Anyway . . I think they're the wrong size . . .

ERIC . Go in the bedroom and try them on . . . I'll come with you . . .

JOYCE. Don't be daft, man . .

ERIC. Go on . . Joyce . . Let yourself go . . Have a bit of fun . . .

JOYCE. Do you want a cup of tea . . .

ERIC. No . . I don't want a rotten, bastardin', bloody, effing cup of
    bloody tea . . . . . Are you not glad to see us back safe and sound . .

JOYCE. Yes . . I'm very glad. I'm relieved . . .

ERIC. That's good . . .

HELEN (*to* AUDIENCE). I was sorry for both of them . . . then . . .
I stayed in the scullery as long as I could . . to leave them alone . . .
One time . . . It looked as if it was going to be alright with them . . .

JOYCE. If you just give us a day or so . . Eric . . To get used to you

ERIC. All right . .

Joyce. I'm just a very funny character . . You know that . . . Just
don't keep pushing us . .

ERIC. Alright . . It's okey dokey . . . You're still my sweetheart, aren't
you?

JOYCE. Yes.

ERIC. That's alright then . .

(*To* AUDIENCE.) And they all bloody came back then . .
The Coalman with a new bit of music . . . He couldn't *wait* to try
it . . .

That certain night, The night we met . . There was magic abroad in
the air . . . etc . . .

HELEN. Norman came into the scullery . . .

NORMAN. Brought you a present . .

HELEN. Me?

The song continues.

NORMAN. Just some scent . . In Parrish's shop . . .

HELEN. Ta . . That's nice . . . I've never used scent very much . .
Evening in Paris . . Lovely bottle . . Isn't it . .

NORMAN. Fancy going out some time . . Two of us . . .

HELEN. *Me* . . . ?

NORMAN. I don't need to go back till tomorrow night . . .

HELEN. Where to like . . .

NORMAN. Meet you in the town . . I know Eldon Square . . . You
know Eldon Square . . Could meet you there . .

HELEN. If you *want* . . .

NORMAN. Do *you* want . . ?

HELEN. I don't mind . . . .

(*To* AUDIENCE) That bloody song the Coalman was singing . . .

And him looking at us . . . I had this feeling . . Like I was in one of them films . . With all the music playing . . . .

GEORGE.   The moon that lingered over London Town . . etc . . .

HELEN (*to* AUDIENCE). I went into the kitchen . . Joyce and Eric were sitting there . . . Not looking at each other . . The Coalman was singing his bloody heart out . . . Both of them had this really sad look on their faces . . .

GEORGE. Poor puzzled moon . . He wore a frown . . . etc . . .

HELEN. Norman kept looking at me . . Nobody had ever looked at us like that before . . In my whole life . .

Up song.

Scene Three

Yours
12 August 1940

ERIC *and* JOYCE *tangoing* . . . . .

GEORGE.   Yours till the stars lose their glory,
                    Yours till the birds fail to sing,
                    Yours to the end of life's story,
                    This pledge to you dear, I bring.
                    Your's in the grey of December,
                    Here or on some far distant shores,
                    I've never loved anyone the way I love you,
                    How could I? When I was born to be,
                    Just your's . . .

                    . . .   This night has music,
                                The sweetest music,
                                It does something with my heart,
                                I hold you near me,
                                Oh darling hear me,
                                I have a message I must impart . . .

ERIC. Come on and dance, Helen . . . Come on . .

JOYCE. Helen doesn't dance, Eric man . . . It's her foot . . .

HELEN I *can't* dance . .

ERIC. Come on . . .

HELEN. I can't . . .

JOYCE. Leave her alone . . .

GEORGE.   Yours till the stars lose their glory, etc . . .

HELEN (*to* AUDIENCE) . . . That was the one thing that got us about my leg being bad . . . I couldn't dance . . . Ee . . I was really jealous of Joyce . . the way she could dance with Eric . . . It was the one thing I was jealous about . . . Lasses being able to dance . . . .

That day . . Anyway . . I couldn't settle on anything . . . I was dying to get to Eldon Square to see Norman . . If he was coming . . . He was supposed to be getting twenty four hours leave . . . But with all the air raids . . we'd heard all the leaves were cancelled . . . Even Eric was called back to his camp, that day . . . And he was only on training soldiers . . . This telegram came . . Ee . . My heart was in my mouth . . . I thought something had happened to Norman . . . . It was just calling back Eric . . . . He tore it up . . . in the stupid way he always carried on . .

ERIC. I didn't get that telegram . . . Did you see us get a telegram . . . Joyce . . . Just bloody got here . . and they're shouting for us to come back . . .

MAM. Hitler's due, Eric, pet . . Any minute . . .

GEORGE. If we're depending on Eric to stop the bugger, he'll be arriving at the Central Station, first thing tomorrow morning . . .

MAM. Don't *say* that, George, man . .

JOYCE. Eric . . . Don't be daft . . . . If it says you've to go back . . . You've to go back . . .

HELEN (*to* AUDIENCE). You could see . . . She was relieved she hadn't to spend the night with him . . .

ERIC. I've just bloody got here . . .

MAM. I'll make you a scrambled egg and toast and onions . . Have we got an onion, Helen? . .

HELEN. Got an onion . . .

MAM. And a cheese sandwich for the train . . .

HELEN (*to* AUDIENCE). And then the Old Soldier comes in with all his gear . . and the cat basket . . and a baby's gas mask . . .

GEORGE. Here he comes . . Britain's Secret Weapon . .

ANDIE. August 14th . . . it's in the papers . . He's arriving in London . . . Adolf . . . Am I right? . . . you not read the papers . . .

GEORGE. *(with the papers).* Wrong . . . August fifteenth . . . It's only the thirteenth today . . So you've two days . . And he'll take another day from London to Newcastle . . .

ANDIE. It's all over . . Bar the shouting . . . Next year, this time, we'll all be singing Deutschland Uber Alles . . and speaking German . . I've always meant to learn a foreign language anyway . . .

JOYCE. Helen . . You speak to him . . He's going to end up behind bars . . . You are . . .

ANDIE. Have you got me ration books, Peggy . . . I'll need me ration books . . .

MAM. Where's he going? Where are you going, man . . .

ANDIE. Not bloody staying here for Hitler to find us . . . I'm going to Wooler . . .

ERIC. He's not coming . . That's defeatist talk, Mr. Ryan . .

GEORGE. If the whole British army's dancing around with their lasses like you, son, I wouldn't be too bloody sure.

ANDIE. I want me ration books, Peggy . . .

MAM. Sid down, you daft old bugger . . I'm making everybody scrambled egg sandwiches . .

ANDIE. That's another thing . . Once I'm in Wooler . . I'll get some real eggs . . Gets on yer nerves that egg powder . . .

ERIC. I just got here, Mr. Ryan . . . It's not right . . Is it . . . Ten minutes after I get here . . They send this telegram ... . Six months . . man . . Since I've seen me wife . . isn't it . . .

ANDIE. That's up to you . . isn't it . . . To work out if it's worth getting shot for . . .

ERIC. Who's getting shot? . . .

GEORGE. That's right . . King's regulations . . Desertion of post . . .

ANDIE. You get some insects like that . . . Don't you . . . They die, soon as they've mated . . It's worth it to them . . Dying . . For a night of love . . . Can't understand it meself . . Never been worth all that to *me* . . . What about *you* George? . . .

HELEN *(to* AUDIENCE*)* . . . And just as me Dad was trying to work

that out, the bloody sirens sounded . . . He jumped into action . .
Put on his Warden's helmet . .

GEORGE. Right . . Everybody into the shelter . .

MAM. The shelter's bloody flooded, man . . I'm not going in there . . .
And I'm sure it's a nest of rats . . . I definitely saw a rat there . .

ANDIE *has produced a baby gas mask.*

GEORGE. What's *he* doing? . . What's that you've got . . .

ANDIE. Just something I picked up . . .

GEORGE. Everybody in the shelter . . .

MAM. I don't care if a bomb strikes us down here and now . . . I am not
going into that rat hole . . .

GEORGE. That is a *Baby Respirator* . . . Where did you get it from? . . .

ANDIE. . . . I picked it up . . . It's for Tibbie, man . . .

GEORGE. That's Government property . . That's for *babies* . . .

ANDIE. I'm telling you . . a man got us it . . . For a banjo . . Me old
banjo . . . I gave him . . .

GEORGE. You gave him away that old banjo . . . . *I* wanted that
banjo . . .

ANDIE. I'll get you another one . . .

HELEN (*to* AUDIENCE) . . . . We could hear from the coast . . The
Anti Aircraft guns starting up . . . Me Mam turned white . . .

MAM. Eee . . Dear Jesus . . I'll never see this war out . . . I know
that . . . .

GEORGE. That's Black Market . . . You know that . . You can be
charged on two counts . . . Listen . . I've warned you . . Get into
your air raid shelter . . .

MAM. George . . Where are you going man . . The bombs are falling all
over the place . . .

GEORGE. I'm Block Warden . . Amn't I . . . I've me duty . . .

ANDIE. It was not Black Market . . I am opposed to all black
marketeering . . I gave me banjo for it . .

GEORGE. Two counts . . . In an emergency . . . The authorities have
powers to shoot you for less than that . . . You are robbing some
innocent baby of a respirator . . .

ANDIE. He got *two* . . Chap that sold us it . . . Said he'd lost one . . . I asked him to get hold of one for me cat . . .

GEORGE. Give me that respirator!

ANDIE. What you want us to do . . . Stand by and let me cat be gassed to a slow death . . . Have you ever seen anybody gassed, you stupid bugger . . .

GEORGE. As Block Warden, by virtue of the authority given to me, I order you to give me that respirator . .

ANDIE. Go and have a shit to yourself, Geordie Stott . . .

MAM. They're going to get the church, this time . . I know it . . . Listen to them . . .

HELEN. That's just the guns, Mam . . .

MAM. I know . . . In me heart . . You know how I know them things . . . like I knew Mrs. Wilcox was going to pass away that week . . .

HELEN. She *didn't* pass away, Mam . . .

MAM. She twisted her ankle, didn't she . . . In the blackout . . . That church is going to get it . . . I know . . . And it's *my* fault . . .

GEORGE. Are you going to give me that respirator . . . ?

ERIC. Will I take it from him, Mr. Stott . . .

GEORGE. I'm the Warden here . . . Even soldiers . . . Take orders from the Civil Defence . .

ERIC. Do they? . . .

GEORGE. Right . . Leave it at that . . . I'm not going to fight over it . . . I am reporting you . . .

HELEN (*to* AUDIENCE). I felt really let down . . . I was sure now . . . Norman would never get away from Tynemouth . . . They'd have them all at the battery . . . It was just like . . . the whole day collapsed round us . . . That had never happened to us before . . Planning a day on somebody else . . Seeing somebody . . . I mean . . . We'd just go to the Leazes Park and watch the ducks . . . and go to the Balloon Barrage and talk . . .

GEORGE. I'm taking down your name . . .

ANDIE. Shouldn't ye be getting to your post . . ?

ERIC. You not think we might be better in the shelter . . Mrs. Stott . . .

MAM. Eee . . I don't know where we should be son . . God only knows . .

JOYCE. Maybe . . If you prayed to Our Lady . . Mam . . .

MAM. Ee . . I *can't* man . . That's the trouble . . . I can't look her in the eyes . . .

JOYCE. Mam . . What's the matter . . .

MAM. Don't *ask* . . . Joyce . . . Don't ask . . . I can't tell you . .

JOYCE. Helen . . Our Mam's upset . . . Look at her . . .

HELEN. What's the matter, Mam . . .

MAM. I don't know what's the matter . . . Are you making the egg . . .

ERIC. If we're not going to the shelter . . I wouldn't mind a sandwich . . .

MAM. Eee . . I don't know where I am . . . Make him a sandwich . . .

ANDIE. Get to yer post, man . . .

GEORGE. I'm putting down your particulars . . . Put down this address . . .

ANDIE. Put where the hell you like . . . I'll be in Wooler . . Before you can do anything about it . . .

GEORGE. You're not taking that gas mask to Wooler . . . It was in the papers this morning . . . A woman got two years for feeding bread to the sparrows.

ANDIE. I'm not feeding bloody sparrows . . . I'm protecting cats from poison gas, man . .

HELEN (*to* AUDIENCE) . . . Then the planes started coming over . . .

MAM. Where are you going, man?

GEORGE. I've got my responsibilities, Peggy . . . I'm Block Warden . . .

MAM. I don't want you to go out . . . I've got a feeling . . . Will you listen to us . . . .

ANDIE. It doesn't matter . . Peggy, man . . . what happens . . . nothing matters . . . . In the end . . . All that's left's the grass . . Isn't it . . . That's all . . . That's what I'm saying . . . It's not worth getting all that worked up about . . .

ERIC. This air raid . . Could last for hours . . Couldn't it . . . I'll say I missed my train . . .

MAM. Ee . . That's a bomb . . Isn't it . . George . . Is that a bomb . . . ?

JOYCE. You said you were up for stripes . . Eric . . . . . If you start going about disobeying orders . .

ERIC. You not want us to stay tonight?

JOYCE. Yes . . I want you to stay tonight, Eric . . What do you think . . .

ERIC. What are you arguing about then . . .

ANDIE. She doesn't want you shot for deserting your post . . .

ERIC. I'm not deserting . . am I . . . I'm just having one night's decent sleep in a decent bed . . . with my wife . . .

JOYCE. Getting into all that trouble . . For one night . . .

ERIC. You not miss us when I'm away . . . When I'm away? . .

JOYCE. Yes . . . I miss you . . . Da' . . stop pushing us . .

GEORGE. I've got to get to my post, Joyce, man . .

HELEN (to AUDIENCE). In the end . . . A bomb fell really near us and we all ran for the shelter . . . Granda . . leading with his cat basket . . .

GEORGE. Have you got to bring that bloody cat with you . . . Hurry up, man . . .

MAM. Look at it . . . It's up to your ankles . . .

GEORGE. I've brought me wellies . . Put me wellies on . . .

MAM. Eee . . I hate that miserable shelter . . .

GEORGE. Did you bring a candle . . Helen . . . Where's a candle . . .

HELEN. I've got a candle . .

ERIC. If you're not bothered . . Me staying tonight . . I was doing it for you . . . All right . . Okey dokey . . . I'll go off . . soon as the All Clear's here . . . I'll go now . .

JOYCE. Eric . . Stop fighting with us . . . There are more important things to worry about just now . . .

GEORGE. Right . . . I'll be back soon as I can . . .

MAM. No . . . *(holding him.)*

GEORGE. Let go of us . . . Helen . . man . . Tell her . . I've got to go to my post, Peggy . . . You knew that . . when I signed up to be a Warden . . . I've got my duties . . .

MAM. Yer first duties yer wife and children . . .

ANDIE *makes to go.*

MAM. Where are you going, *now*, Da' . . .

ANDIE. I've left her gas mask . . Tibbie's gas mask . .

ERIC. They're not gassing today, Mr. Ryan . .

ANDIE. I'm taking no chances, son . .

GEORGIE. Will you stay put . . . Bloody shrapnel's flying all over the place . . .

ANDIE. Give us yer tin hat . . then . . Till I get the mask . .

HELEN. *I'll* get it, Granda . . . I'll make a flask of tea for people . . .

MAM. Helen . . Will *you* stay put . . .

GEORGE. Nobody is leaving this shelter . . .

HELEN. Let me get him the mask, Da . . . And I'll make some tea . . .

GEORGE. I've got to get to my post . . .

MAM. I don't want any tea . . .

ERIC. I wouldn't mind a cup of tea . . .

   Bomb.

MAM. Listen to that . . .

ANDIE. I want that *mask* . . Ye bugger!

GEORGE. Right . . I'll *get* yer bloody mask!

ANDIE. You're a gentleman, George . . .

ERIC. Soon as the All Clear's come, I'll go . . . You think I'd better go, Mrs. Stott . .

MAM. Ee . . . It's no use asking me . . . My nerves are up to high Doh, pet . . . I don't know what anybody should do . . .

JOYCE. *Go* back in the *morning,* then . . . If you have to . . .

MAM. Joyce . . will you stop fighting . . . I can't stand it . . On top of everything else . . .

GEORGE. There's yer bloody mask . . . But ye're not taking it to Wooler . . .

ANDIE. I've got yer mask, pet . . Don't worry . . Ye'll be alright . . . I know he doesn't understand a bloody word . . But I *do* . .

GEORGE. Can I go to my post now . .

MAM. No . .

HELEN (*to* AUDIENCE). Then the planes were on top of us . . A wave of them . . . The whole shelter was like vibrating with the noise of them . . . Me Mam was moving her lips . . . You could read her praying . . Her eyes shut . . Saying the same words over and over again . . . Into herself . . . Then the bombs began to drop . . . At first away from us . . Then closer . . .

MAM. They've got the church . . I know it . . George . . That was the church . . . They've got . . . I know . . .

GEORGE. Nowhere near the church . . . Take it easy lass . . .

MAM. *Nothing* is safe . . . Even the house of God . . . What am I going to do, Helen . . What am I going to do, for God's sake . . .

HELEN. Mam . . . It's alright . . It'll be alright, Mam . . .

Bombs.

MAM. You don't know the half of it . . It's me . . . It's all *my* fault . . .

ANDIE. If that's all your fault . . Peggy, man . . All I can say is . . I never knew you had it *in* you . . .

HELEN. Granda . . shut up a minute . . .

GEORGE. Here . . I brought some lemonade . . . Give her a sip of lemonade . . .

ERIC. Christ . . . That was a near one . . .

MAM. I know . . . . . They've laid it flat . . . The whole church . . . Everything's been destroyed . . . Father Kennelly's and the other fathers . . .

GEORGE. Will I go and see . . .

MAM. Stay here . . . For God's sake . . .

GEORGE. It's quietening down a bit . . .

ERIC. I'd go . . But I haven't me steel helmet with us . . . And there's all that shrapnel . . .

MAM. George . . Lend Eric your helmet . . .

GEORGE. Let *me* go, man . .

HELEN. Stay here, Da . . She's upset . . .

JOYCE. Will I come with you . . ?

ERIC. Don't be daft, Joyce . . What do you want to come with me for . . .

MAM. You're wasting your time, Eric . . I know . . . It's down . . I know . . .

GEORGE *pulls out his mouth organ and plays 'Hang Out The Washing'.*

ANDIE. Tell ye what . . Give us the Last Post . . .

JOYCE. Granda . . For God's sake . . .

ANDIE. I like it on the mouth organ . . Yer Da' plays it beautiful . . Somebody's bound to have had their number up them bombs dropping . . .

GEORGE. Here's a good one . . You like this one Andie . . . You are my sunshine, My only sunshine . . .

ANDIE. That's a good one . . . *(Joining in.)*

GEORGE.   . . . The other night dear,
              As I lay dreaming . . . *(Breaks off.)*

What the hell's that smell . .

ANDIE. What smell . .

JOYCE. God . . They're not dropping gas . . . And Eric's out there . . .

ANDIE. He's got his mask . . .

GEORGE. Not bloody gas . . .

MAM. I can't smell anything . . . I'm too upset . . .

GEORGE *sniffing, traces the smell to the cat.*

GEORGE. It's that bloody moggie . . He's shit himself in his basket . . .

JOYCE. He has . . . It's horrible . . .

MAM. Get it out of here . . Will you . . . Dad . . .

ANDIE. It's a natural thing . . . I don't know what you're all making such a song and dance over it for . . Happens to everybody . . everybody shits . .

GEORGE. Not in bloody cat baskets. . .

ANDIE. What else can he do . . . You want us to fit it out with a flush lavatory . . . ?

GEORGE. Just get him out, man . . .

ANDIE. In that . . .

HELEN (*to* AUDIENCE). There was just going to be another fight . . .
About throwing out Tibbie . . when the All Clear sounded . . . .
Eee . . I was so happy . . . I could go down to see if Norman was
coming . . . . Even if he wasn't . . Just going down to Eldon
Square . . sitting on our seat . . . . Me Mam came into us . . When I
was in the kitchen . . . She shut the door behind her . .

MAM. Listen, Helen . . On Sunday . . After Mass . . Father Kennelly . .
You know how they stand at the door . . as you go out . . He said to
us: He couldn't help seeing us saying the Lord's Prayer . . . You
could see . . He'd never seen anybody say it like that before . . . Like
I believed in it with my whole body and soul . . .

HELEN. You do, Mam . . .

MAM. I haven't finished, yet, man . . He touched us . . the back of my
hand . . . Standing there in his lovely priest's vestments . . You know
what I mean . . And the light through the glass windows . . That
picture of Jesus . . The light was coming through the windows . . .
Shining on his face . . . He touched my hand . . It gave us a funny
feeling . . You know what I mean . . . You probably wouldn't . . *
Joyce would . . But I couldn't tell Joyce . . . I don't want Joyce to
hear this . . . You listening to me Helen . .

HELEN. I *know* what you mean, Mam . .

MAM. It was a real sinful thought . . . The feeling was sinful . . . And I
never told him at Confession . . . How could I? . . It was him that
was in the Confessional . . Father Kennelly . . . But that feeling . .
It was like sometimes when you hear a choir and an organ bursting
into a lovely hymn . . . Or you go in the park . . on a lovely summer
day . . . It made us really feel glad to be living . . . Looking at his
face . . and knowing there was such a person in the world . . .

HELEN. That's not sinful, Mam . . . Don't be daft . . That's lovely . . .

MAM. It is, Helen, man . . . You don't know the half of it . .

HELEN. It isn't . . It's lovely . . . It is . . . You're a daft bloody soul . . .
But some of the things you come out with . . . They're lovely . . .

MAM. I'll help you with the supper . . .

HELEN (*to* AUDIENCE). Then Eric came back . . with Joyce . . .
She'd gone out to look for him . . Frightened he'd been hit by a
bomb or something . . They came back . . . Looking a bit more
together . . .

ERIC. Yes . . I might as well stay . . I got on the 'phone to the station . .
The train I'd have to get . . . I'd miss my supper . . .

MAM. What about the church . . God . . I forgot all about it for the minute . . . *(Going to the window.)*

ERIC. It's alright . . Mrs. Stott . . . Some shrapnel's gone through the roof . . and a couple of windows have been blown in with the blast . . .

MAM. Thank God . . Dear God . . Thank God . . . for saving us, this day . . Amen . . . It's not the one with Jesus in the Cross . . .

ERIC. I never noticed, Mrs. Stott . . .

MAM. Just two windows . . ?

ERIC. Two or three . . .

MAM *(to* HELEN). There you are . . You see . . That's me being warned . . .

JOYCE. About what, Mam? . . .

MAM. Just been warned . . that's all . . By God . . .

GEORGE.   Yours till the stars lose their glory . .

MAM. Get away, man . . I'm trying to make the supper . . .

GEORGE.   Yours till the birds fail to sing . . . etc . . .

  ERIC *and* JOYCE *tangoing.*

HELEN *(to* AUDIENCE). I couldn't stand watching them any longer . . I got me coat . . and ran off to Eldon Square . .

MAM. Helen, pet . . You haven't had anything to eat . .

HELEN *(to* AUDIENCE). He was there . . Waiting for us on our seat . . . But he was huddled up . . . Not moving . . . I thought maybe he'd been there since the raid . . and some shrapnel had hit him or something . . .

HELEN. *(Shaking him gently)* . . Norman . . . Are you alright . . . Norman . .

NORMAN. All Clear . . .

HELEN. For hours . . .

NORMAN. I've got twenty four hours leave . . . Been up five nights running . . . They gave me twenty four hours leave . . .

HELEN. You should've come up to the house . . . If you were tired . . .

NORMAN. I like meeting you here . . I'm alright, now . . . Just settled in with a sandwich and a lemonade . . and the siren started . . Couldn't budge . . . I was finished . . .

HELEN. Will I take you home for a rest? . . .

NORMAN. I've twenty four hours leave . . First twenty four hours we've got together . . isn't it . . . We've got a whole twenty four hours . . . I know . . . Could've been . . . I put my helmet on . .

HELEN. You look a bit daft in it . . . Take it off . . .

NORMAN. What are we going to do . .

HELEN. If I 'phoned them . . I could maybe get tomorrow off . . . I could work extra time Thursday and Friday . . .

NORMAN. You look nice . . .

HELEN. Don't be daft, Norman . . .

NORMAN. You *do* . . . Do you always have your hair pinned up . . ?

HELEN. It's easier . . It gets in a mess . . . if I let it loose . . .

NORMAN. Let's see . . .

HELEN. Don't be daft, man . . People are watching . . .

NORMAN. Nobody's watching . . . Nobody here . .

HELEN. We could go to the pictures . . You like Charlie Chan . . . Charlie Chan's on at the Welbeck . . .

NORMAN. Go on . . Let it down . . I'm telling you . . I know . . It'll suit you . .

HELEN. It'll just be a mess . . I know . . There you are . . I told you . . .

NORMAN. It's lovely . .

HELEN. You don't need to say these things to us, Norman . . I keep telling you that . . .

NORMAN. It's lovely . . . Your hair's really lovely . . .

HELEN. Will we go up to the Leazes . . .

NORMAN. Listen . . . Let's go daft . . eh . . Come on . . . I feel like it . . . I want to go to the Oxford . . . Tonight . . With you . . .

HELEN. Norman . . man . . . . That upsets us . . . Don't keep pulling us to dances . . . . I hate that . . .

NORMAN. I want to dance with you . . . What's the matter with your *leg,* anyway . . . It looks alright to *me* . . . Sometimes, you can hardly notice you limping . . . can you?

HELEN. Something to do with one leg being shorter than the other . . . They noticed it too late for us to get an operation . . . It doesn't bother me . .

NORMAN. A waltz you could do easy . . . I can see . . the way you walk . . . We'll just do the slow dances . . .

HELEN. Norman . . I couldn't, man . . Honest . . I wish you wouldn't talk about it . . .

NORMAN. It is . . Your hair's lovely like that . . .

HELEN (to AUDIENCE). He was making us feel funny . . . The way he was looking at us . . . I couldn't believe it . . I'd get a lad like him . .

NORMAN. Tell you something . . I think I'm really falling for you . . . Do you know that . .

HELEN. You're just trying to get round us . . Will we go over to the park . . .

NORMAN. I promise . . If you hate it . . after the first ten minutes . . . We'll go out . . . Just try it with us . .

HELEN. Why have you got to dance with us . . . I don't understand you Norman . . .

NORMAN. I want to take you to a dance . . That's all . . . It's like faith healing . . You know? . . I'm making your leg better . . .

HELEN. That's a good idea . . .

(To AUDIENCE) . . . . And he puts his arms round us . . . I could smell the soap on his skin . . One of his brass buttons dug into my neck . . But he was lovely . . . The way he kissed us . .

(To NORMAN.) . . How does that cure my leg, then, Norman . . ?

NORMAN. Faith . . . I told you . . Look you're walking better . . Look . .

HELEN. I'm not . . . I don't feel it . . . Am I? . .

(To AUDIENCE.) Ee . . he had me as daft as himself . .

Up Dance Band.

That certain night, the night we met,
There was magic abroad in the air,
There were angels dining at the Ritz . . .
And . . .

NORMAN. . . . A nightingale sang in Eldon Square . .

HELEN (to NORMAN). Ten minutes . . And if I hate it by then . . . I'm going home . .

NORMAN. It's one, two, three . . One together . . Left together . . Right together . . It's easy . . . A waltz . .

HELEN. I know a waltz . . I've watched our Joyce doing it enough
times . . . Come on, then . . . Let's get it over with . . . If I stand on
your feet . . Don't blame us . .

NORMAN. That's not a waltz . . It's a slow foxtrot . .

HELEN. I've watched Joyce doing that, too . . .

Up Band.

> I may be right and I may be wrong,
> But I'm certainly willing to swear . .
> There were angels dining at the Ritz,
> And a nightingale sang . . .

NORMAN.   . . . In Eldon Square . .

HELEN. See what I mean . . I'm useless . .

NORMAN. You're dancing . . Look at you . . .

HELEN. I can keep time with the music . . . That's easy enough . . .
But look at us . . .

NORMAN. Helen, love . . You're dancing . . Look at you . . . You are . . .

HELEN. I'm not . . I'm just moving with the music . . . I'm not
properly dancing . . .

NORMAN. You are, Helen . . . You dance fantastically . . . Honest . . .
I don't say things to you . . You know that . .

HELEN. It's just that sherry . . . It's got us so I don't know where I
am . . Norman . . .

NORMAN. That's the secret then . . . Every time we go to a dance . . .
we'll fill you up first . . . .

HELEN. You think I *am* dancing?

BAND.   When dawn came stealing up, all gold and blue,
> To interrupt our rendezvous,
> I still remember how you smiled and said,
> Was that a dream or was it true,
> Our homeward step was just as light,
> As the tap-dancing feet of Astaire,
> And like an echo — far away . . .

NORMAN & HELEN.
> A nightingale sang . .
> Its voice really rang . . .
> A nightingale sang . .
> In Eldon Square . . .

HELEN (*to* AUDIENCE). Eee . . We stayed right to the end . . . I'd never been so happy in my life . . . I suppose I wasn't dancing properly . . And my ankle began to hurt a bit . . But just the whole crowd . . Being together . . Moving with everybody in the whole crowd . . . And that last waltz . . .

Up Last Waltz.

. . . Just dancing it, it came to us . . (*to* NORMAN). Norman . . Have you somewhere to stay tonight?

NORMAN. I'm staying with you . .

HELEN. You see Eric's back . . . Otherwise you could've come back to our house . . . Where are you going to go . . ?

NORMAN. I love you . . Do you know that? . .

HELEN. I've no idea why . . .

NORMAN. I've got twenty four hours . . I don't want us to be separated . .

HELEN. I'll be sleeping with me Granda in the same room tonight . . When Eric's home . .

NORMAN. One of the lads . . Says there's hotels . . In Jesmond . . Always got rooms . .

HELEN (*to* AUDIENCE). . . We ended up at this Private Hotel off Osborne Road . . . It had a Vacancies notice outside . .

(*To* NORMAN). There you are . . You'll be all right here . . I'll come over in the morning for you . . .

NORMAN. Helen . . I don't want you to leave me, love . .

HELEN (*to* AUDIENCE). I couldn't stand leaving him either . . .

(*To* NORMAN.) I've got to get back to Walker, Norman . .

NORMAN. You can't go away from me now . . . How can you do that . . . I've only got twenty four hours . . .

HELEN. I'll come over and have breakfast with you . . .

NORMAN. I don't mean you to stay in the same room with me . . . If we got rooms next to each other . . . That would be good . . . Just under the same roof . . .

HELEN. Norman . . You're daft . . . That sherry's still affecting you . . .

NORMAN. Come on . . It looks a nice clean place . .

HELEN (*to* AUDIENCE). . . You see . . What it was . . I really trusted him . . He was a really good person . . . It was the first time I felt I could give myself to somebody else like that . . Trusting him . . .

(*To* NORMAN.) . . Me Mam's waiting for us, Norman . . . If I didn't come home . .

NORMAN. Where are you going? . .

HELEN. Let go of us, Norman . . will you . .

NORMAN. I told you, you could dance . . .

HELEN (*to* AUDIENCE). We must've been talking louder than we thought . . Because the wife from the hotel opened the door and asked us what we wanted . . . I have no idea, to this day, what came over us . . Because I just said:
. . . We want a room for tonight . . . A double room . . . Yes we're married . . . The wife looked at us . . And said something like 'That's up to you' . . . Norman couldn't say anything . . . He was so surprised . . . We just signed the book . . . And went upstairs . . . The wife said she could maybe give us a spam sandwich and a cup of tea . . . I was really starving . . . We had it in our room . . . It was nice . . Nice chintzy curtains and matching bed cover . . .

NORMAN. I didn't mean you to come in the same room . .

HELEN. I know that . . . It's a lovely room, isn't it . . Clean and fresh . . .

NORMAN. She's put a hot water bottle in the bed . . . Bit dry — the sandwiches . .

HELEN. They're alright . . . I phoned me Dad's Warden Post . . They're going to tell him . . .

NORMAN. I wasn't trying anything on . . . You know that, Helen, love . . .

HELEN. I know, Norman . . .

NORMAN. But I love you . . .

HELEN. I love you . . .

NORMAN. Will I sleep on the chair then . .

HELEN. If you want . .

NORMAN. I don't mind . .

HELEN. Don't be daft, man . . (*Taking his hand and kissing him.*) . . . I trust you . . You trust me . . We trust each other don't we . . .

(*To* AUDIENCE). . . . I didn't even have a nightie with us . . I had
to go to bed in my petticoat . . . It was a good job I'd borrowed
Joyce's . . . It was a nice yellow one . . . And we didn't do
anything . . in the night . . or the morning . . . We kissed and cuddled
a bit and went to sleep with our arms round one another . . . It was
lovely . . . Having his arms round us . . . Going to sleep . . . and waking
up . . . with him beside us . . . And the sun shining through the
curtains . . .

Bring up 'Yours'.

> Yours to the end of life's story,
> This pledge to you dear, I bring,
> Yours in the grey of December,
> Here or on far distant shores,
> I've never loved anyone the way I love you,
> How could I,
> When I was born to be
> Just yours . . .

Lights fade.

End of Act One

Act Two

Scene One

The Lovely Weekend
November 1942

GEORGE.　　I haven't said thanks for that lovely weekend,
　　　　　　Those two days of heaven you helped me to spend,
　　　　　　The thrill of your kiss as you stepped off the train,
　　　　　　The smile in your eyes like the sun after rain.

JOYCE.　　To mark the occasion, we went out to dine,
　　　　　　Remember the laughter, the music, the wine,
　　　　　　That drive in the taxi, when midnight had flown,
　　　　　　Then breakfast next morning, just we two alone . .

GEORGE.　　You had to go, the time was so short,
　　　　　　We both had so much to say,

JOYCE.　　Your kit to be packed, the train to be caught,
　　　　　　Sorry I cried but I just felt that way.
　　　　　　And now you have gone, dear, this letter I pen,
　　　　　　My heart travels with you, till we meet again,
　　　　　　Keep smiling my darling,
　　　　　　And some day we'll spend,
　　　　　　A lifetime as sweet as that lovely weekend . . .

HELEN.　　*(with her rosary).*
　　　　　　. . Hail Mary, holy Queen, Mother of Mercy,
　　　　　　Hail our life our sweetness and our hope,
　　　　　　To thee do we cry, poor banished children of Eve,
　　　　　　To thee do we send up our sighs,
　　　　　　Mourning and weeping in this vale of tears.
　　　　　　Turn then, most gracious advocate,
　　　　　　Thine eyes of mercy towards us,

And after this, our exile,
Show unto us the blessed fruit of thy womb, Jesus.
Oh clement, oh loving, oh sweet Virgin . . .
Pray for us, oh holy mother of God,
That we may be made worthy of the promises of Christ.

(*To* AUDIENCE.) . . . The week me Mam went to London . . . for her Auntie's funeral . . . I stopped going to Mass . . . I still said my rosary . . . I always felt better after saying it . . . I'd given up going to Confession, months ago . . . I had to confess to adultery with Norman . . . and I didn't believe I *was* committing adultery . . . I wasn't . . . But the whole thing blew up that weekend . . . Me Mam came back from London . . . The Coalman was organising a party . . . He was always having parties . . . from then on . . . Everything began to turn . . . Rommell had been beaten in Africa . . . and papers were all full of it . . . Pictures of Monty . . . and the tanks in the desert . . . Me Dad was in trouble, too, with me Mam . . That was the week he'd joined the Communist Party . . . At the yard . . .

It started with us finding this flat . . . For Norman and me . . . In Elswick . . Clifton Road . . .

NORMAN. It's nice . . I like it . . .

HELEN. Norman, love . . I don't want you to feel I'm pushing you or anything . . Do you hear me . .

NORMAN. I know, Helen . . .

HELEN. I'm not pushing you to marry us or anything, Norman . . . I mean that . . . I'm just sick of having nowhere of our own . . . It'd be lovely . . wouldn't it . . Having a weekend together in our own place . .

NORMAN. Helen . . Look . . . I'm sorry . . . I love you . . .

HELEN (*to* AUDIENCE). When he came out with it at last . . . I felt that I'd known all the time . . I wasn't angry with him . . . I could understand how he hadn't been able to tell me . . . It wasn't *his* fault, anyway . . . It was me pushing him . . .

NORMAN. I mean . . I was just a kid . . when I married her . . .

HELEN. It's all right, Norman . . Honest . . .

NORMAN. I love *you* . . I bloody hate that . . . Hurting you like this . . I couldn't help it . . .

HELEN. It's alright, love . . Only thing that gets us . . Is you spending your leaves with her . . That's all . . . It's understandable . .

NORMAN. I'll spend the next one with you, Helen . . I mean . . If there's a next one for us to spend together . . . I mean . . . If you don't finish with us . . .

HELEN. Norman . . Why should I finish with you . . . I love you . . .

NORMAN. What are we going to do?

HELEN. I bought some Ginger Beer and Pasties . . . To see what it felt like . . . Eating in our own house . . .

NORMAN. I tried . . you know . . Dozens of times . . To tell you . . . Just stuck in my throat . . .

HELEN. You've told us now . . . Do you want a pasty . . . ?

NORMAN. Bloody hated it . . You know . . Telling you lies . .

HELEN. I know you did . . Will I scratch your eyes out or something . . To make you feel better . . Put your coat down . . .

(*To* AUDIENCE.) . . We sat on his greatcoat on the floor . . . It was a cold November afternoon . . . But the sun was out . . . Coming through the windows . . .

(*To* NORMAN.) . . I got a lipstick in Parish's . . 'Evening in Paris' . . . 3/8d. it cost us . . . You like it . . ?

NORMAN. I mean . . . I was nineteen . . so was she . . . When we got married . . .

HELEN. I'll tell you one thing, Norman . . If you really don't want me to kick in your teeth, love . . I don't really want to hear any more about you and her . . Just now . . . I know all I want to know . . . now.

Up 'The Cossack Patrol'. GEORGE singing it.

HELEN (*to* AUDIENCE). . . Eee . . My poor Mam . . She came back full of it . . From the joys of London . . And found her whole world collapsing round her . . .

JOYCE. Helen . . Come in me room a minute . . I want to talk to you . . .

GEORGE. Wait a minute, man . . She hasn't had a drink yet . . . What's his name hasn't had a drink yet . . . What are you going to drink, Comrade . . .

HELEN. What's happened to me Mam, Da . . .

ANDIE. She's been kidnapped by the German High Command . . .

HELEN. Where's me Mam . .

JOYCE. Helen . . I want to talk to you . . .

GEORGE. I went to the station . . . Three hours late . . The train from London . . I'll go back in an hour . . We'll all go back . . . The Old Soldier's getting married again . . Has he told you . . .

(To NORMAN — with books.) . . There you are, then . . . You take them back to your camp, son . . Hand them round the other lads . . . If you want . . I'll send somebody over to sign you all on . . . Could you get a better system, son . . 'From each according to their ability, to each according to their need.' . . .

ANDIE. Beautiful words . . Only thing to touch it's the Sermon on the Mount . . .

GEORGE. Talking about real politics now, Andy, man . . Not your opium of the masses.

Listen . . What will I give you for a wedding present . . I'll play the organ for you . . will I? . .

ANDIE. I'll let you be Godfather at me first christening, son . . .

HELEN. Granda . . You're not getting married, are you . . Eee . . He's not . . .

JOYCE. He's just answered an advert in the Chronicle about a woman with a spare room . . . That's all . . .

ANDIE. Sixty-eight . . . Deaf . . . Wants a bit of company . . . Frightened of the air raids . . . Five bob a week . . . I'm getting bloody sick of getting pushed from pillar to post every bloody day . . . It's upsetting Tibbie . . . She needs a settled home . . doesn't she . .

JOYCE. Are you coming to help us with the sandwiches? . .

HELEN (to AUDIENCE). Into the scullery into more problems . . .

JOYCE. I'm bloody pregnant . . Helen . .

HELEN. That's nice . . I'm really happy . . .

JOYCE. For Christ's sake . .

HELEN. Do you not want to be . .

JOYCE. What do you think . . . I don't know whose it is . . Helen, man . . .

HELEN. It's Eric's . . .

JOYCE. I'm trying to work out . . when Eric was last on leave . . Was it the last leave . . He only came for the day . . ?

HELEN. Was there all that many . . You can't work it out . . .

JOYCE. If Eric stayed the night his last leave, I'm alright. One of his last two leaves . . he just spent the day here, remember?

HELEN. I'm trying to think on . .

JOYCE. It was an Air Force lad . . Ian . . He was really cannie . . from Scotland. We just fell into it. That was the first time . . . . I'll tell you something . . . I don't know how it was but it's the first time I've enjoyed myself with a lad.

HELEN. Did you not use protection . . .

JOYCE. We just fell into it . . I'm telling you . . . Eee . . What can I do, Helen . . . Can I get rid of it? . . .

HELEN (*to* AUDIENCE). . . . . And then me Mam came in . . Full of it . . . a load of parcels in her arms . . . In her funeral costume . . .

MAM (*to* GEORGE). Where were you, man? . . . I'll talk to *you*, after . . Ee . . Helen . . Joyce . . The time I've had . . . I'll show you what I've got . . . Hullo Norman . . .

GEORGE. I stood in that bloody freezing station . . over an hour, Peggy . .

MAM. After bringing you a present . . I went all over London looking for something nice for you . . .

GEORGE. Did she *leave* you anything? . .

MAM. I didn't go for her to leave me anything . . I went to pay respects to me Da's sister . . . They were asking for you Da' . . Everybody . . .

GEORGE. He's too busy . . . Getting married . . .

MAM. Eee . . He's not . . . Da . .

GEORGE. What did she leave you . .

MAM. She left me Da her piano . .

ANDIE. That's nice of her . . Bring it with you . . Did you?

MAM. Eee . . You should've seen me and yer Auntie Marge . . . In this Rolls Royce . . Going to the funeral . . . Joyce . . . You know what your Auntie Marge is like when she's had a sherry . . . She was putting her hand out the window . . Like the Queen . . Waving, to the crowds . . . Look at this cake . . The shops are full of them . . .

HELEN (*to* AUDIENCE). She started emptying her bag . . Full of all kinds of rubbish . . It was a shame for her . . . The cream cake . . had

that artificial cream in it . . Like Zinc Ointment . . . And she'd
bought some pies . . and they'd turned in the train . . . The only
decent thing she'd bought was some material . . .

MAM. The black market there . . All over the place . . . What do you
think of that . . . There's a dress length for you and Joyce there . .
isn't there, Helen . . .

JOYCE. Mam . . We can't wear the same dress, man . . Can we . . ?

MAM. *I'll* wear it then . . There's yer present, George . . . I got you
some tobacco . . for making cigarettes, Da . . It's somewhere . . .
I've got a London paper, Norman. Would you like to look at it . . .

NORMAN. Thanks Mrs. Stott . . .

GEORGE. There's yer sherry, Peggy, man . .

MAM. I don't want sherry, at this time of day . . .

GEORGE. It's a party . . . Celebrating Tobruk . . and you getting safe
back from the battlefield . . . Prosit!

JOYCE. Mam . . Do you remember when Eric was last home on leave . . .
For the day — was it last time or the time before . . ?

MAM. The mistake was to let your Auntie Marge take anything before
the funeral . . . You should've seen her at the cemetery . . . I didn't
know where to look . . . She had a fit of the giggles . . . just as they
were laying the poor soul to rest . . . Eee . . The policeman . . There
was this lovely policeman . . Six foot tall . . . We got lost near
Trafalgar Square.

GEORGE. Peggy . . . I might as well tell you this straight away . . .

MAM. It really upset us . . You not being there at the station . . . It was
a let-down . . Bob was there . .

GEORGE. Bloody would be . .

ANDIE. This isn't meant as an offence to you, Peggy . . . But I saw this
in the Chronicle . . Room offered for reasonable charge . . .

GEORGE. I'm bloody trying to tell her something . .

HELEN (*to* AUDIENCE). Then me Mam noticed Norman with all
them Communist papers . .

MAM. Did *you* bring them into this house, Norman?

JOYCE. When did our Eric come home on leave, Mam . . For the day?

ANDIE. So I went up . . Just out of curiosity . . It's in Heaton . . . Just
beside the library . . and the park . . .

MAM. Norman . . You know the Communists do not believe in God . .
Them's Communist papers . . . Do you know that . . . Anti-Christ . .

HELEN. They're not his, Mam . . .

JOYCE. The last time . . . Did he stay for the weekend . . ?

MAM. Are you not going to open your present . . ?

GEORGE. I'm opening it . .

MAM. I don't know what your religion is . . But they're the Anti-
Christ . . The Communists . . That's why they're losing the war in
Russia . . .

GEORGE. They're *winning,* the war, man . . It's all Stalin pulling the
wool over Schickelgruber's eyes . . .

MAM. I must say I didn't think you were one of them . .

HELEN. It's not *his* papers, Mam . . .

GEORGE. I'm showing you something . . .

MAM. Are you not going to open yer present . .

GEORGE. I'll bloody *open* it . .

MAM. If that's the way you're going to take it . . Give it me back . . .

GEORGE. I didn't mean that, Peggy . . .

ANDIE. So I goes up to Heaton . . . This wife opens the door . .
Cannie . . Clean . . Stone deaf . . . Come in answer to yer advert in
the Chronic . . . I says . . . Nice day . . she says . . Her batteries had
gone in her deaf aid . . and she was waiting for more to come in . . .

JOYCE. Mam . . I want to know when Eric was last here . . .

MAM. He's *your* bloody husband . . .

GEORGE. *(opening the parcel).* That's lovely . . That . . Ta . . Cannie . .
(Looking at them unsure what they are.)

MAM. They're cuff links, George . . .

GEORGE. I know what they are . . . Here's a kiss for them . . .

MAM. George, man . . Don't be daft . . Act yer age . . . Where's me
calendar . . .

ANDIE. So I writes it down . . . On a pad . . . What I'm doing there . . .
Takes a long time to have a conversation writing things down . . .

MAM. What's he talking about? . . Da . . what are you rambling on
about . . ?

ANDIE. I'm going to the Heaton widow's . .

MAM. What for? . .

GEORGE. He's telling you . . .

MAM. Eric came on leave from Pickering . . didn't he . . The last time . .
He got his Corporal stripes . . He looked nice in his stripes . . didn't
he, Helen . . . That's right . . . It was a Wednesday, he came wasn't
it . . . Didn't have to go back the same day to Pickering.

JOYCE. Wasn't that the time before, Mam?

MAM. I'm looking . . .

GEORGE. It's a Party card . . . I know what I'm doing . . . My position
on the Shop Stewards' Committee . . . I had to join the party . . .
Peggy . . .

MAM. What's he talking about, now . . .

GEORGE. The Communist Party . . . I'm a Communist . . .

MAM. Sit down a minute, man . . I'm trying to work out when Eric was
here . . What do you want to *know* for anyway . . .

HELEN. She just wanted to know . . .

GEORGE. That's my card . . Everybody in the Yard's joining . . .

MAM. George . . . First thing tonight . . You get to the church . . and go
to confession . . . That's what *you've* got to do . . . God in heaven . .
I can't even have three days away from here . . . without everybody
going mad . . .

ANDIE. I'm just going to the widow's . . . Five shillings a week . . . But I
want my ration books, Peggy . . .

MAM. I went to see Old Mother Riley, at the Gloria . . . That time Eric
was here . . . No . . That was September . . .

HELEN. You might as well hear this, too . . Mam . . . While you're at
it . . .

GEORGE. Helen; Leave her alone, just now . . .

HELEN. Me and Norman . . . Mam . .

MAM. Ee . . You're not . . Thank God . . You're getting married . .
That's lovely . . . I can't believe it . . Norman . . . Come here, pet . . .

HELEN. Mam, man . . . .

ANDIE. I want me ration books, Peggy . . .

MAM. Wait a minute, Da . . I can't get over it . . . Norman . . Helen . . Do you hear them . . you have all my blessings . . the pair of you . . I wish you all the happiness in the world . .

HELEN. We're *not* getting married, Mam . . .

NORMAN. Helen . . Do you not think . . you should maybe tell your mother later . . when . .

MAM. I don't understand you . . Do you understand her, George . . ?

ANDIE. She's not getting married . . .

HELEN. We've got a house . . In Elswick . . A flat . . with a garden . . .

MAM. Helen . . What's the matter with you . . . What are you talking about . . .

ANDIE. She's got a house in Elswick . . .

MAM. Da . . Keep out of this a minute . . will you . . .

HELEN. I'm thirty-one, Mam . . . I'm old enough to know what I'm doing . . I'm going to live in Elswick with Norman . . .

MAM. I don't understand her . . I do not understand that girl for one minute. One minute she's saying she's not getting married, the next she is . . .

ANDIE. She says . . .

MAM. *You* keep out of this . . .

ANDIE. Give us me ration books then, and I'll get off to Heaton . . .

GEORGE. Andie . . Take it easy . . . Just take it easy a minute . . . Norman . . . You've lost us here, lad . . . I don't get your drift . . . I do not get your drift, son . . .

HELEN. It was *my* idea, Da . . . It's no use talking to him . . .

GEORGE. I'm bloody *talking* to him . . . I want something straight . . . Have you been messing about with . . .

MAM. Don't start acting the father with her after all them years, George . . Helen, pet . . .

GEORGE. I bloody *am* her father. Am I? Mind *you*. The way things are going, now I'm not sure . . .

MAM. My God. He's not *married*! He's not a married man, is he?

HELEN. Just fell into it young, Mam. He's not *really* married.

MAM. Oh, dear God in heaven. He's a married man

ANDIE. It doesn't matter, Peggy! . . . It'll all be nothing in a hundred years' time . . .

GEORGE. What the hell good does that do . . . We're bloody here *now*, aren't we, man . . *How's* he not married, Helen?

HELEN. He got married very young . . .

GEORGE. Is he a Russian or something . . Does he have to have an interpreter . .

HELEN. I made up my mind . . To go . . This weekend, Mam . . That's the best thing . . A quick break . . If you can lend us some curtains and blankets . .

GEORGE. You see what you're doing, son . . Do you? . . You're breaking up a whole household . . .

NORMAN. I'm very sorry, Mr. Stott . . . I didn't mean . . .

ANDIE. I'm thinking on . . If this Heaton widow doesn't work out . . . That might be the solution . . If I move in with Helen . . In Elswick . . I like Elswick . . There's cannie fish and chip shops there . . You get the best fish supper in Newcastle in Elswick . .

MAM. I just can't believe it . . George . . I cannot believe it . . It's a nightmare . . The whole thing's a miserable nightmare . . .

HELEN. I'll make you a cup of tea, Mam . . .

MAM. Get your coat on . . We're going round this minute, to Father Kennelly . . .

HELEN. I'm not going anywhere, Mam . . .

GEORGE. If he's getting divorced . . .

NORMAN. There's no divorces during the war, Mr. Stott . . .

GEORGE. *After* the war . . . Before the war . . . If you're getting divorced . .

MAM. What difference does that make . . . What God has joined together, nobody can break asunder . . . You know your Bible as well as me . . .

GEORGE. They haven't that problem in Russia . .

MAM. I'm going to take the pair of you to Father Kennelly's . . .

JOYCE. Take me *too*, Mam . .

MAM. Thank God . . I've at least one good child . . . Come here, pet . . .

GEORGE. I'm just saying . . They have places . . You can get rid of your wife . . at the drop of a hat . . . In Russia . . .

MAM. What do they do . . . Put them down . . Like in the Cat and Dog
Home . . . I wouldn't put it past the bloody heathens!

NORMAN. I'm very sorry, Mrs. Stott . . .

MAM. So you bloody should be . . . God in heaven . . We had such a
lovely time . . . at Auntie Linda's funeral . . I was so happy . . In the
train coming back home . . . And look what I've come back to . . .
We've nothing, George . . have we . . . the whole world's collapsed
round us . .

HELEN. Mam . . Don't be daft . . There's yer tea, man . .

MAM. How could you do this to us . . Helen . . You were such a good,
clean, lovely lass . . . How could you do this to me and your
father . . . ?

HELEN. I don't *know*, Mam . . .

MAM. I remember now, Joyce . . . When Eric was last here . . He'd got a
lift in a lorry from the camp . . He had to go back the same night . . .

JOYCE *buries her face in her hands.*

HELEN (*to* AUDIENCE). They didn't believe I was going . . Till the
Sunday . . When I came into the kitchen . . with my cases and
things . . . I felt a bit easier . . because Joyce's period suddenly
came . . . It was a false alarm . . . So that was one problem less, me
Mam had to face . . .

GEORGE. (*at the piano*).
            You'd be so nice to come home to,
            You'd be so nice by the fire,
            When the breeze on high,
            Sings a lullaby . . . etc.

MAM. Where are you going, pet?

HELEN. Mam . . Don't start that all over again . . .

MAM. Helen . . You can't leave us . . man . . In the middle of a war . .
and everything . . Helen . . Pet . .

HELEN. I'll come over and see you every day . . From me work,
Mam . . .

MAM. George . . Our lass is going away . . .

GEORGE. It's that bloody Lost Boy's fault . . Bringing the Tailor's
dummy home . . . like that . . . Told you . . first time I saw him . .
We'll have nothing but trouble from that stupid swine . .

MAM. Are you not even staying for your dinner, pet?

HELEN. I've got to get to the house and arrange everything . .

MAM. I'll never step over your doorstep . . You know that . . . I swear that . . .

HELEN. Ta ra . . Da' . . . Ta ra . . Mam . . . I'm sorry I couldn't have had a nice white wedding for you in St. Anthony's . .

MAM. Don't Helen . . I can't even bear thinking about it . . .

HELEN (*to* AUDIENCE). I rushed out the house . . Another minute and they'd have me crying too . . . But me Mam came after us . . .

MAM. You forgot yer Ration Book . .

HELEN. Ee . . I did . . .
(*To* AUDIENCE.) Taking it from her . . . It was a funny feeling . . . Like it was the final break . . from her . . . It was funny taking that ration book . . . It was harder to do than anything I'd done up till then . . .

MAM. Will you go to Mass, tonight . . . For me . . ?

HELEN. Alright . . I'll go . . .

MAM. Is there a shelter in yer place . . ?

HELEN. It's a good one . . Better than ours . . An Anderson . .

MAM. Thank God for that . . !

GEORGE. You'd be so nice to come home to . .
You'd be so nice by the fire . . . . etc.

HELEN (*to* AUDIENCE). A funny thing happened . . When we were sitting down . . . To our dinner . . Norman had got some haddock . . . One of the lads in the unit had been fishing off the pier . . It was lovely . . . We were just sitting down to have it . . . when the bells started ringing . . All over Newcastle . . .

NORMAN. Did you put it in the Sunday Sun . . . ?

HELEN. I must've done . . . Is it the invasion . . ?

NORMAN. Can't be the invasion, Helen . . They sound too cheery . . . It's a peel . . . They'd be sounding the sirens . . wouldn't they . . .

HELEN (*to* AUDIENCE). We went outside . . It was cold . . . Norman put his arms around us . . . when he noticed I was shivering . . .

NORMAN. I'll tell you what it's for . . . It's for Tobruk . . . It's victory bells . .

HELEN. Eee . . It is . . Listen to them . . .

(*To* AUDIENCE.) We stood in the doorway . . Listening to the bells ringing out all over Newcastle . . . It was like a sign for me and Norman . . I felt it was . . And it was the first time . . I felt any hope

(*To* NORMAN.) . . I feel that, now . . Do you? . . Things are turning . . . We're going to beat them, at last . . . The Germans . . . We're going to be all right!

NORMAN. It's a good sound that, isn't it . .

HELEN. Come on . . . Our haddock'll be getting cold, love . .

Up 'So Nice to Come Home to'.

Scene Two
The White Cliffs of Dover
6 and 7 June 1944

GEORGE.   There'll be bluebirds over,
            The white cliffs of Dover,
            Tomorrow, just you wait and see,
            There'll be love and laughter
            And peace ever after,
            Tomorrow, when the world is free.
            etc . . .

MAM. Helen . . Yer Da's been hit by a bomb . .

HELEN. Eee . . he hasn't, man . . .

MAM. He's in the General . . . I can't face going up to see him on me own . .

HELEN. I was just going to wash me hair, Mam . . Wait — I'll get a coat on . .

MAM. That raid before . . Did you get it . . . Just one bloody plane got through . . . And it had to get your Da . . .

HELEN. I'm just coming, Mam . . .

MAM. To think we've gone all through the war without a scratch . . . And it had to happen now . . . Dear God. Helen . . say your rosary on the way . .

HELEN. I'll say it, Mam . .

(*To* AUDIENCE.) I hadn't got me rosary . . or even me Missal . . . It had got lost years back . . . I don't know what the plane was doing over Newcastle . . It was D Day . . . and you'd have thought the Germans would've needed all their planes over in France . . .

(*To* MAM.) Did they say how bad he was, Mam . . ?

MAM. I didn't dare ask, man . . . I wouldn't care . . But I'd just come in from Mass and Confession . . .

HELEN. I thought he was on day shift, Mam . .

MAM. I'm telling you . . It happened at the Yard . . . Have you got yer torch . . . ? Eee . . When I saw the policeman at the door . . . He was firewatching at the Yard . . It was his night . . . He was a good Da to you . . wasn't he . . Whatever you say about him . . He was a lovely Da . . .

HELEN. He'll be all right, Mam . . .

MAM. And a good man to me . . . Couldn't get a better man . . .

HELEN. Is Joyce at work . . ?

MAM. I don't know where anybody is . . . Dear God . . A thing like that to happen to us . . .

HELEN. It'll be alright, Mam . . .

MAM. How can it be alright . . . For God's sake . . The poor man's been struck by a bomb . . .

HELEN (*to* AUDIENCE). It couldn't have been a very big one . . Because when we got to the hospital . . They told us he'd gone home . .

M AM. Gone home . . . It's George Stott . . .

HELEN. They said that was right . . .

MAM. He's been in an air raid . . . A bomb hit him . . .

HELEN (*to* AUDIENCE). We tried to get a taxi straight back to Walker . . Me Mam was sure they'd made a mistake . . And he'd died on the road . . .

HELEN (*to* AUDIENCE). When we got back . . Joyce was fighting with Eric, who was telling her how he'd lost his stripes . . .

ERIC. I've told you, man . . I was in trouble . .

JOYCE. What trouble . .

HELEN (*to* AUDIENCE). . . . . And me Granda had turned up, with his problems . . .

ANDIE. Helen . . I want to talk to you . . . That spare room you've got in Elswick . . .

MAM. Is he not here? . .

JOYCE. Who's not here? . .

MAM. I told you . . didn't I . . They've lost him . . They made a mistake . . and they're trying to cover up . . . Da' . . . He's gone . . He's passed away . . . The Germans got him . . . I've just come from the General . . . A bomb hit him . .

HELEN. Stop panicking . . Mam . . Joyce make a cup of tea . . will you . .

ERIC. You're an old soldier, Andie, . . aren't you? . .

ANDIE. Who's hit by a bomb . . George has never been hit by a bomb, has he? . .

JOYCE. Eee . . He hasn't, has he, Mam?

ERIC. How would he be hit by a bomb, man . . If he was hit by a bomb . . He'd be smashed to smithereens . . Bits of him would be blown across to Gateshead . .

MAM. For God's sake . . Tell your man to hold his rotten tongue . . .

ERIC. I'm just saying . . what would happen if he was hit by a bomb . . amn't I? . . .

JOYCE. Keep quiet, a minute, Eric, man . . .

ANDIE. Didn't you used to be a Corporal . . .

ERIC. Don't *you* bloody start . . .

MAM. He was firewatching . . I gave him spam sandwiches . . . . for his bait . .

ERIC. *I* wouldn't *mind* a spam sandwich . . .

HELEN. Where are you going now, Mam? . . .

MAM. Going back to the General . . To find me man . . . I've got a right to him . . Whatever state he's in . . Put your coat on, Helen . . . .

ERIC. Them hospitals . . Mrs. Stott . . If they said he's gone, he's gone . . They know what they're talking about . . .

MAM. Ee . . That's what's happened . . They said he was gone . . And we thought they meant he'd left the hospital . . Dear God . . .

HELEN. Mam . . They didn't . . They said he'd left the hospital . . To go home . . .

MAM. I don't remember them saying that . . Did they say that? . . They said he'd gone . . .

HELEN. Went home . . .

MAM. Where is he, then, for God's sake?

ERIC. I don't understand anybody going home after a bomb hitting him . . .

JOYCE. You don't understand anything . . . You don't even know how you lost yer bloody stripes . . .

MAM. Where is he? . . . *(Going.)*

ERIC. Where's she going, now? . . .

ANDIE. Going to have a chat with the Virgin Mary . . . Best thing for her . . .

JOYCE. Helen . . Nothing has happened to our Da . . has it? . .

HELEN. Eee . . I don't know, Joyce . . .

ERIC. Did you say you were making a spam sandwich . . .

HELEN. I don't live here now . . . Better ask your wife, Eric? . .

ERIC. God . . I could, Granda . . You'right there . . .

HELEN (*to* AUDIENCE). Then me Dad came in . . . With a bit of sticking plaster at the side of his head . . . Everybody shut up . . . Like a ghost had walked into the room . . . The Old Soldier spoke first . .

ANDIE. It must've been a *smallish* kind of bomb, Geordie . .

MAM. Eee . . George . . Are you alright, pet . . . Where have you been . .

GEORGE. Give us a seat, somebody . . . will you . . . Helen, make us a cup of tea . . .

MAM. Do you want some brandy? . . . We've been all over Newcastle looking for you, pet . . . Haven't we Helen?

GEORGE. I could do with some brandy . .

JOYCE. Are you alright, Da . . .

GEORGE. Three weeks ago . . He knew the clock on Newcastle Town Hall was two minutes slow . . Lord Haw Haw . .

ANDIE. George . . She's getting ideas . . . The Black Widow . .

GEORGE. Two nights ago . . Lord Haw Haw . . Did you hear him? . .

MAM. Is that all they did to you . . . I mean . . Have you any internal
injuries, George . . They haven't damaged any of yer insides . . .

GEORGE. He says . . Lord Haw Haw . . 'The Communists and Jews
are kidding themselves. Germany's beaten . . . Germany is stronger
than ever . . . '

ERIC. Bloody bluff . . You should see the stuff we've been loading
(Stops himself.) . . . I'm not supposed to say anything about it
anyway . . . You didn't hear that . . Did you?

ANDIE. Is that how you lost yer stripes . . .

ERIC. I lost me stripes because they took us for a spy . . .

GEORGE. Do you not want to hear about my encounter with
Hitler . . Fair enough . .

MAM. We're listening, man . . But you keep on about bloody Lord Haw
Haw . . .

GEORGE. He warned the Communists and the Jews . . to watch out . . .
It's well known the Communists are strong in the Neptune Yard . . .
We sell more Daily Workers there than anywhere else in the North . .

MAM. May God forgive you . . .

GEORGE. Up Uncle Joe . . Right, Eric?

ERIC. Up the Ruskies . . .

GEORGE. They showed them what for in Stalingrad . . Didn't they . .

MAM. You ask him, Helen . . . Is he damaged inside . . .

GEORGE. I'm telling you, woman . . . I was up there . . . on the roof . .
fire watching . . .

MAM. Did you eat yer spam sandwiches . . .

GEORGE. I did, they were very nice . .

JOYCE. Mam . . I want to know how Eric was taken for a spy . .

GEORGE. I'm up there . . That warning sounds . . . Are you listening
to us . . . Leave the bottle here, man . . I've had a terrible shock . . .

MAM. I'm just pouring meself one . . .

GEORGE. Now . . . Here's the thing . . . I'm standing up there . .
Alert . . Looking out for incendiaries . . bombs . .

MAM. I said a special prayer for you at Mass tonight . . Did you know
that . . . That's what protected you . . . And I said a prayer over
your sandwiches . . .

GEORGE. I'm standing there when in comes this Heinkel . . Right . . .

ERIC. Down in Sussex . . They thought my Tyneside was a German accent . . that's all . . . Okey dokey . . ?

JOYCE. No . . It isn't okey dokey . .

GEORGE. This Heinkel . . You could see him . . He was looking for something . .

MAM. For you . . .

GEORGE. Looking for the *Yard*, man . . . You could see . . He was going backwards and forwards . . . Look . . If they know Newcastle Town Hall clock's two minutes slow . . They'll know all about the whole communist cell in the Yard . . . They might even've been after me as Party Secretary . . . Wouldn't put it past them . . .

ERIC. From up there . . Mr. Stott . . They couldn't make out *who* you were from there . . .

GEORGE. They dived . . I'm telling you . . . A hail of bullets at us . . . They were so low . . I could read the number on the wings . . See that bloody swastika . . . Diving straight at us . . . I threw me stirrup pump at him . . . Take that you bastard . . ! Then I retreated . . Down the ladder . . . Me helmet dropped off . . . In the heat of the fighting . . .

ANDIE. First rule of a soldier . . Hold on to your rifle and your helmet . . .

GEORGE. That's how they got us . . . A bullet bounced off the wall . . Got me here . . See . . .

MAM. Dear God . . Thank you . . Thank you, dear God . . For bringing my man back to us . . I'm going to put thanks to the Secred Heart in the Catholic Herald this week . . I am . .

GEORGE. Stunned us . . . Next thing I knew . . I was in the General . . Some lass putting a plaster on me head . . . I showed the bastards. Eh . . Eric . . son . . .

GEORGE. One thing . . anyway . . son . . . Right . . . Nobody can say, when it's all over, *I* haven't done my bit for the old country . . .

HELEN (*to* AUDIENCE). It would've been alright . . If we'd had out supper and went to bed . . But me Dad had to drag us all out to the pub on Welbeck Road . . to celebrate . . . And that's where the trouble started . . . Eric went for the drinks . . Me Mam and Da' sat at the table . . When he came back . . He had only two pints . . . I didn't want one anyway . . . As soon as me Mam saw that . . . She stood up . . Pulled me Da' up too . . . And walked out the pub without speaking . . .

ERIC. It was queuing up . . Mrs. Stott . . .

HELEN (*to* AUDIENCE). Eric tried to hold her back . . But she was off . .

ERIC. The chap in front of us . . . I'll get you yer drinks . . . I got mixed up . . .

JOYCE. Eee . . Eric . . What have you done now . . .

ERIC. I wouldn't deliberately not get yer Mam and Da a drink, Joyce . . would I . . . Look (*showing them his money*) . . . I've got plenty of money on us . . .

JOYCE. Where did you get all that . . . ?

ERIC. It was about her . . I was only defending her . . This chap in front of us . . . He made a nasty remark about yer Mam, man . . I'm telling you . . .

JOYCE. Like what did he say? . .

ERIC. A nasty remark . . .

JOYCE. Maybe he was a spy like you . . .

ERIC. For Christ's sake . . I'm telling you . . . They did . . bloody think I was a spy . . . That's how I ended up losing me stripes . . . I got picked up in Sussex . . At a dance . . That's all . . .

JOYCE. At a *dance?* What were you doing at a dance? . .

ERIC. What do *you* do at a dance . . .

JOYCE. That's what I *mean* . . .

ERIC. You know what it's like . . Before I know it . . . . They've got this policeman . . And I'm getting the third degree . . who I am . . and where I come from . . and then the bloody M.P.'s turn up to take us back to the camp . . Drunk and disorderly . . and losing a rifle . . I left me rifle in the bog . . That's all that happened . . .

JOYCE. That's all . . You go gadding about looking for lasses in dances . . while I'm stuck here all on me own . . That's very nice . . . Now I know where I stand . . .

ERIC. What do you mean . . You know where you stand . . I like dancing . . You know that . . You don't deny us a bit of a dance now and then . . *You* know there's no harm in it, Helen . . .

JOYCE. We'd better get back to our Mam, Helen . . .

ERIC. Helen, man . . .

HELEN (to AUDIENCE). . . Back in the house . . It was Battle Stations . . Me mam was sitting there, at the table . . Her arms folded . . . Black . . . The Coalman was at the piano, hiding from the storm . . .

ANDIE. I'm just telling yer Mam, Helen . . She wants us to get married . . . On August Bank Holiday . . . The black widow . .

MAM. I have seen some mean, some miserable characters in my day.. . But my God! . . . I never thought my own son-in-law —

ERIC. Bloody let us tell you . . .

MAM. Joyce'll tell you . . . Whenever he was due home on leave . . I saved our meat ration . . . and points . . and everything . . I said: I want that lad to come home to a decent meal . . I even saved cigarettes for him . . . Every time he came back, there was twenty Woodbines on the mantlepiece waiting for him . . . . Is that right, son?

ERIC. I'm just telling you what happened . . .

MAM. Am I telling you a lie . . . Tonight . . Everybody was having heart and onion pie . . . What do you sit down to . . .

ERIC. This bloke in the pub . . .

MAM. Pork chop and apple sauce . . . Because I know . . A lad who's been away fighting for his country wants to come home to a nice, cheerful, tasty meal . . .

ERIC. Look . . I'm telling you . .

MAM. I was even saving up coupons for his birthday . . Did you know that, Da?

ANDIE. What you're asking for is people not to be people, Peggy . . That's where you're falling down . . . Gratitude . . That's not people . . It would be very nice if people were grateful . . and human beings and that kind of thing . . But that's not how they're made . . . People are not human beings . . . That's where you go wrong! . .

MAM. I don't care so much for myself . . But after his wife's father . . . Has been snatched from the jaws of death . . .

ERIC. It slipped me mind . . in the heat of the minute . . That's all . . . If you'd have waited another second . . I would've . . .

MAM. I just cannot understand anybody like that . . .

ANDIE. Take that Black Widow . . . I've given her five bob a week since I moved in . . . Cleaned and lighted her fire every day . . . Brushed her shoes . . . After I've done with them . . And then she pays us by wanting to marry us . . . .

MAM. It was even *him* that suggested we go out for a drink . . .

HELEN (*to* AUDIENCE). . . It just got too much for Eric . . . He stuck his hands in his pockets . . and threw all his silver and copper on to the table . . .

ERIC. There's yer bloody drink, you rotten old cow! . . . Bloody fill yerself up till it comes out yer rotten throat! (*going.*)

JOYCE. Eric . . Where are you going . . .

MAM. Dear God . . Listen to him . . . I never thought I'd ever hear foul language like that under my roof . . George, man . . . . Are you not going to do anything about it . . .

GEORGE. I've had a bad day, Peggy, man . . . I've nearly been killed . . . It's beginning to hit us now . . . . I think I should go to bed . . .

MAM. Eee . . Pet . . Yes . . . I'll make you a bottle . . .

HELEN (*to* AUDIENCE). Eric came back with his pack and a case . . .

JOYCE. Eric . . . Where are you going . . .

ERIC. Going back to Sussex . . . That's where I'm going. Where I'm wanted . . . I'm not staying in this shithouse any longer . . .

MAM. My God . . Look at the filth coming out of his mouth . . .

ERIC. Are you coming? . .

JOYCE. Where, like . . in the middle of the night . . .

ERIC. We'll get a room somewhere . . . For the night . . .

MAM. Now . . Everybody has witnessed that . . . I did not drive him out of my house . . . .

ERIC. Will you shut yer trap you filthy old papist bag . . .

MAM. There you are . . . I told you . . . Never marry out of yer faith . . Sooner or later he's going to come out with it . . .

ERIC. I'm talking to my bloody wife . . . Shut yer bloody gob, man! . . .

MAM. George, man . . .

GEORGE. Take it easy, son . . .

ERIC. Are you coming? . . .

JOYCE. You can stay here and apologise to me Mam . . . But I'm *not* running off with you Eric . . . Not after what I've heard tonight . . . Finding out what you're up to, when you're away from me . . .

ERIC. How do I know what *you're* up to . . like . . When *I'm* away . . . All these bloody Yanks all over the place . . .

JOYCE. What do you mean by that? . .

ERIC. Funny thing . . You're never short of stockings . . are you . . Where do you get them from . . What have you got to do to get them . .

JOYCE. Bloody take that back . . Hear me!

MAM. What are you hinting at, Eric . . .

ANDIE. I must admit . . Peggy . . If I was a lass . . The way them Yanks go about . . Throwing their dollars all over the place . .

MAM. Keep out of this, Da . . Will you . . . Are you insinuating . . .

ERIC. Oh, go and have a shit to yourself . . . The lot of you!

HELEN (*to* AUDIENCE). And he walked out . . . Right out of our lives . . .

ANDIE. Now . . . Eric's not staying . . With me complications with the widow . . You understand . . You think you might take us back for a few weeks . . Till I find somewhere else . . I was going to ask Helen . . But I can't take to Elswick . . somehow . . I mean . . If you've been in Walker all yer life . . . I've nobody to talk to . . in Elswick . . I don't like the library, either . . .

HELEN (*to* AUDIENCE). Joyce . . Stood there . . White . . Looking at the door Eric had gone through . . .

JOYCE. I don't bloody care . . I don't care . . I don't care if he *never* bloody comes back! . . .

GEORGE.   The shepherd will tend his sheep,
            The valley will bloom again,
            And Jimmie will go to sleep
            In his own little room again.

            There'll be bluebirds over,
            The white cliffs of Dover,
            Tomorrow, just you wait and see . . . etc . . .

HELEN (*to* AUDIENCE). On the next morning, the Wednesday, it was on the wireless. They'd landed in Normandy . . They were already miles and miles inside France . . . But all I could think of was

meeting Norman, that night . . He was going to try to come back for
the evening from Durham . . . We hadn't seen each other for weeks .
weeks . . . When he was away . . . Sometimes I couldn't stand it . . . .
I was packing his other tunic . . to take to him . . That morning . .
He could go right back to Durham . . . And I saw he'd left some
papers . . and his pay book . . in his tunic . . . . Eee . . I said to
myself . . He's a careless bugger . . . Doesn't even look after his pay
book . . . I just looked inside . . I don't know why I looked . . . And
it bloody hit us . . . His wife's name was there . . who he was paying
his marriage allowance to . . and then . . . an allowance to one
child . . . . I kept going back to the page . . To make sure .,. I
couldn't believe it wasn't a mistake . . . But it was there, right
enough . . . . One Child . . Matthew Peter . . . . I washed up the
dishes . . . And went into Parsons . . . I just went through the day . . .
I was acting full of it . . . The lasses in the Blade shop said to us . .
What had come over us . . . I was so cheery . . . I couldn't bear to go
home to me Mam's . . . .Instead . . I went to the station . . to wait
for Norman's train . . . If he was coming . . . Waited for hours . . .
Men kept looking at us . . . Especially the Yanks . . . One of them
offered us a bar of chocolate . . I just stared right through him . . .
In the end . . I gave up . . I went to our bench in Eldon Square . . .
And he was bloody there . . Sitting on our bench . . .

NORMAN. I came on an earlier train . . I didn't know what to do,
love . .

HELEN. I brought yer tunic . . .

NORMAN. Ta, love . . You alright . . ? I can stay to the eleven
o'clock train . . . We've got them now, haven't we . . . Couple of
months and we'll finish the bastards . . . . Are you alright, love . . ?

HELEN. Norman . . I want you to tell me about the kid.

NORMAN. About the kid? . . .

HELEN. I don't understand it . . . I thought you just stayed with your
father and mother when you went back to Birmingham . . .

NORMAN. Helen . . I'm sorry, love . . .

HELEN. I didn't mean to look in your Pay Book . . . I just looked
automatically . . .

NORMAN. I'm sorry . . . I don't know what happened . . .

HELEN. How old is he? . .

NORMAN. He's nearly two . . .

HELEN. Two . . .

NORMAN. Eighteen months or so . . . That week I went back . . It was a bad week . . Birmingham was really getting it . . . I just went to see her . . . She was all on her own . . . I mean . . It was me that had brought her to Birmingham . . She didn't know anybody there . . . I didn't want to hurt you, love . . .

HELEN. A little boy . . Matthew Peter . . .

NORMAN. *She* named it . . .

HELEN. Do you love him? . . .

NORMAN. I don't know . . . I just felt sorry for her . . . On her own . .

HELEN. So you bloody gave her a kid . . .

NORMAN. I know . . .

HELEN. You *don't* bloody *know* . .

NORMAN. I love you . . . You know that . . . .

HELEN. I don't know anything, Norman . . I know I bloody love you . . . What did you need to go back to her for . . . Could you not finish with her . . . Once and for all . . For her sake . . .

NORMAN. You know me . . I'm a bloody idiot . . Amn't I . . . I'm just one of these characters . . . That mess up their own lives . . . and everybody that come in contact with me . . .

HELEN. What good does that do . . . Beating your bloody breast about it!

NORMAN. I love *you*, Helen . .

HELEN. *Do* you? . . .

NORMAN. What do you want to do? . .

HELEN (*to* AUDIENCE). And suddenly . . I felt really weak . . I hadn't eaten anything all day . . . I suddenly was dying for something to eat . . . I've got some sausage meat . . .

NORMAN. Yes . . . We'll go home . . .

HELEN (*to* AUDIENCE). I looked at him . . . Trying to get behind his eyes . . .

NO (*to* NORMAN). Do you love me? . . . I don't *know*, Norman . . .

NORMAN. I *do*, Helen . . .

HELEN (*to* AUDIENCE). There was this scent from the flowers in the Square . . and the birds were shouting away at the top of their voices . . .

NORMAN. Bloody racket, these birds are making!

HELEN. They do that, before they go to sleep . . .

NORMAN. Do they? . . I'm sorry, love . . I should've told you . .

HELEN. Yes, well . . You couldn't . . No use saying that . . . You couldn't tell us . . .

NORMAN' It just happened . . It doesn't make any difference between us . . . Honest . . It doesn't . . .

HELEN. Doesn't it . . . Come on . . . We'll go back to Clifton Road and have something to eat . . . Before it's time for your train . . .

NORMAN. Do you forgive us . .

HELEN. What does *that* mean?

NORMAN. Do you?

HELEN. I'm not bloody God, am I . . . . Just don't talk about it just now, Norman . . .

(*To* AUDIENCE.) It was such a lovely night . . . Warm . . And all the trees fresh green . . . with their new leaves . . and the birds singing . . And everybody round us happy and full of it . . . And the sight of him . . Looking so miserable . . . dejected . . and guilty . . . I couldn't help it . . .

(*To* NORMAN.) Come here . . You stupid idiot . . . (*Kissing him lightly.*) . . . I still love you . . . I can't help it . . . I wish you hadn't done it but, love . . .

NORMAN. I know . . .

HELEN. You *don't* bloody *know*, Norman . . You don't bloody know the *half* of it, love . . . .

Up 'The White Cliffs of Dover'.

Scene Three

A Nightingale Sang in Berkeley Square
8 May 1945

GEORGE. I'm going to get lit up,
    When the lights go on in London, etc.

The sound of hooters coming from the Tyne . . .

MAM. Look! I got a brown loaf at Jackson's . . .

HELEN (*to* AUDIENCE)..The hooters were all screaming
away . . . For V.E. Day . . Everybody was smiling and talking to
each other in the streets . . . Joyce was sorting out the bunting . . .
And me Mam chasing all over Newcastle looking for bread . . .

MAM. Do *you* fancy trying for a loaf, Helen, pet . . .

HELEN. I'll go in a minute . . . Mam . . .

MAM (*to* HELEN). What's he doing there . . . ?

GEORGE. I'm making the guy . . . For the bonfire tonight.

MAM. Is that Hitler?

GEORGE. That's not Hitler . . No . . Hitler's dead . . . Forget about
Hitler . . .

MAM. Where did you get that bowler?

GEORGE. It's me old bowler . . . From me wedding . . .

MAM. You're not going to burn that?

JOYCE. What should I do about Eric, Mam?

HELEN. One of these days, Joyce . . . You'll actually make your own
mind about something, won't you?

JOYCE. I'm just asking . . .

MAM. Give me that hat . . .

GEORGE. I *need* it . . . That's yer Capitalist . . . You burn
capitalism . . . That's the idea . . That's the whole point of the
war . . . Isn't it . . Finish the old system . . once and for all . .

JOYCE. Did you read *his* letter?

HELEN. I read his letter . . .

JOYCE. What do you think? You see, he's due in about an hour.
Shoud I go and meet him . . ?

HELEN (*to* AUDIENCE). That week . . . Eric had written her . . .
First time since he walked out of our house . . .

JOYCE. It was a nice letter, wasn't it . . .

HELEN. Yes . . . It was all right . . .

(*To* AUDIENCE). 'Dear Joyce, I'm coming back from Sussex on
eighth at six o'clock . . If you want to meet us at the station . . .
Hope you are keeping well . . Eric . . '

He was going to put 'love' . . but you could see he'd had second thoughts . . .

JOYCE. I mean . . . For *Eric* to write a *letter* . . *You* know him, Mam . . .

MAM. Meet him, if you want to . . Is nobody going out to see if they can get some more bread . . .

JOYCE. Mam . . . You see . . . I thought we were finished . .

JOYCE. Would *you* come with us, Helen? . . .

HELEN (*to* AUDIENCE). Then the Old Soldier turned up . . . with his cat and his gear . . .

GEORGE. Is that cat still living Andy . . . he'll be due his old age pension, now . . . won't he . . .

ANDIE. I'm here . . .

MAM. What's the matter? . . .

ANDIE (*to* GEORGE). How's the Hero, eh . . . ?

GEORGE. I mean . . . You've got to hand it to us . . We've done it haven't we? . .

MAM. Da' . . . What are you doing here, with your cases and Tibbie?

ANDIE. You asked us, woman . . . When I saw you in Shields Road the other day . . . I was touched . . .

JOYCE. I think this time . . If we had a place of our own . . . Like Helen . . . That's what we've got to do . . We're going to find a place . . .

MAM. I meant . . . Come up for a bite or something . . . That's all I meant . . .

ANDIE. I made a mistake . . I'm sorry . .

MAM. It's Eric turning up . . .

ANDIE. Where is he? . .

JOYCE. I'm meeting him at the station, Granda . .

ANDIE. Taking up with him again . . . ?

JOYCE. I don't know . . .

ANDIE. Say you do know, and you'll know. (*Looking at the effigy.*) What the hell's that?

MAM. Well might you ask.

GEORGE. What do you think it is?

ANDIE. Looks like you on yer wedding day.

JOYCE. What do you mean, Granda? Say I know.

ANDIE. I don't know, Joyce. Sometimes I say owt . . First thing that comes into me head . . It doesn't matter in the end, does it, Joyce? He's as good as any other lad, isn't he, Eric? I mean . . He has all his equipment . .

GEORGE. What do you think, Andie . . The dawn of a new world, eh?

ANDIE. Is it?

GEORGE. Wait and see, lad. The people are going to take over the world they fought for. Right, Joyce?

MAM. I'd *like* you to stay, Da . . Us all under the one roof on V.E. night . . But it's Eric . . And not having enough bread . . .

ANDIE. I'll get some bread . . . The widow's got bread.

GEORGE. Peggy . . . Give us back me bowler . . . Look . . . Without the hat . . . It looks nothing . . . Look at it . . .

GEORGE. Peggy, give us back me hat . . .

MAM. Why can't you burn *Hitler* like every other normal person in the country . . .

HELEN (*to* AUDIENCE). . . . I was meeting Norman at the Square . . . He was coming back from Durham . . To spend V.E. night with us . . . We were going to see all the lights . . . and end up at the bonfire in Walker Park . . .
. . . I was really full of it . . Going to the Square . . . The town was packed . . . Lasses at times kissing soldiers . . . or airmen . . and that . . . They were doing something at the top of Eldon Monument . . Putting up torches or something . . To light at night . . . There was bunting all over Newcastle . . .
. . On me way in I even got a white loaf for me Mam . . and one for ourselves . . . I know I was daft . . but that was like a sign . . Everything was going right for us, at last . . .
. . . I didn't twig at first . . . that Norman was carrying a case . . I was before him . . at our seat . . . I just saw Norman . . . The case didn't register . . . Afterwards, I knew he was carrying it, so that I would see it . . . and it would help him to break it to us . . . But all I saw was Norman . . .

(*To* NORMAN:) . . . I beat you, love . . .

NORMAN. Yes . . . I've been to the flat . . .

HELEN. Oh . . . Did you go for a shave and that . . .

NORMAN. Helen . . . I've got to go to Birmingham, tonight . . .

HELEN. Sit down a minute . . . Has something happened, love . . .
There's nothing happened to yer Mam or Da . . Has there?

NORMAN. I'm getting moved to Leicester . . .

HELEN. I brought a flask of tea . . Do you want a cup of tea . . .
and a biscuit . . .

NORMAN. See . . My mother's in a right state . . with Tony . . .

HELEN (*to* AUDIENCE). . . There was only two of them . .
Like Joyce and me . . Tony and him . . . He'd been missing since
Arnheim . . .

(*To* NORMAN:) . . Have they told them definitely . . He's
been killed . . .

NORMAN. He's had it . . . Helen . . You know that . . . . . You
know what happened in that bloody mess . . She's in a real
state . . . I 'phoned them last night . . . I've got leave . . . To go
to her . . . .

HELEN. You didn't tell us you were applying for leave, love . . .

NORMAN. Compassionate leave . . . I've got ten days . . . and
they're moving us to Leicester . . That's near . . you see . . .
To Birmingham . . .

HELEN. Eric's turned up from nowhere . . . Joyce's gone to
meet him . . .

NORMAN. That's good . . . They'll all be coming back now . . .

HELEN. What time's your train, then . .

NORMAN. Couple of hours . . .

HELEN. You're going to miss the bonfire, then . . and everything . . .

NORMAN (*nearly breaking*): . . . I know, Helen . . . I'm going to miss
everything, love . . .

HELEN. What's the matter, pet . . Come on . . What's wrong, . . .
love . . .

NORMAN. I love you . . .

HELEN. I know . . .

NORMAN. Just . . . I'm getting pulled . . . all ways . . .

HELEN. It'll be all right, love . . . I'll come and see you at Leicester . . will I? . . . And when you're demobbed . . .

NORMAN. I'm telling you . . That's it . . Helen . . . I don't know if I'm *coming* back . . . That's what I'm saying . . .

HELEN. You going back to *her* . . . Is that what you mean?

NORMAN. I don't know . . . My mother wants me back . . With what happened to Tony . . . She wants me near her . . .

HELEN. You going back to *her* . . . Are you? In Birmingham . . .

NORMAN. It's not that . . .

HELEN. Do you lover *her* better than me . . Is that what you've found out, Norman?

NORMAN. I don't know what I'm going to do in the end . . . It's the kid . . . isn't it? . . . I love him . . He really needs me . . . You should see him . . . When I'm with him . . . I mean . . . A kid . . he needs a father . . . doesn't he? . . .

HELEN. Yes . . A kid needs a father . . . Yes . . . I suppose he does . . .

NORMAN. In a few months, it'll be clear . . . . . Just now . . . You don't know where you are . . . do you?

HELEN. I know where I am . . Norman . . Yes . . I do . . . I'm clear enough . . .

NORMAN. I don't want to leave you, Helen . . I love you . . . You not see that . . .

HELEN. I don't know what I see, Norman . . . I should've known that . . . shouldn't I . . . I mean . . I should've known . . we weren't going to kind of live together for the rest of our lives . . . I shouldn't have got into thinking like that . . . The two of us should be together till death parted us . . . That was stupid . . . wasn't it . . . You've got things pulling you away from us . . All the time . .

NORMAN. I think . . in the end . . when it's all clear . . I'll come back to you . . . I'll write to you . . . I'll send you an address where you can write to me . . .

HELEN. Do you want some tea? I'm having some tea . . . I was looking forward to walking round the town . . . with all the lights on . . . with you . . . Your train'll be away . . . won't it . . . Before it's dark . . . I've a biscuit . . .

NORMAN. I don't want a biscuit . . No . . .

HELEN. I was even thinking . . now the war's finished . . . If I could have a kid . . .

NORMAN. Helen . . I'm sorry, love . . I bloody am . . .

HELEN. I know . . . It doesn't do any good, does it . . . Me Mam made them biscuits . . They're horrible . .

NORMAN. Give them to the pigeons . . .

HELEN. What'll we do, till your train's due . . . ?

NORMAN. You're really good . . You deserve somebody really good . . . Not a useless rotten bastard like me . . .

HELEN. I said . . I do . . . You're right . . . I might go out and look for somebody now . . . Now I know I deserve somebody worthwhile . . . If Joyce and Eric take up again . . . Should I give them the flat . . . ?

NORMAN. I don't know . . love . . .

HELEN. Come on then, Norman . . Cheer up . . We've won the war, haven't we . . . ?

JOYCE. Helen . . love . . Come here and see what Eric's got for you . . .

HELEN (to AUDIENCE). They were all there . . . the whole family . . . Me Mam was making up the Old Soldier's bed in the kitchen . . . Eric was dancing with Joyce . . .

ERIC (with a banana). I've got a present for you . . There you are . . . Haven't seen one of these for a long time . . . Eh? . . .

HELEN. Ee . . . Where did you get it, Eric . . .

ERIC. Give yer long lost brother a kiss, man . . . Come on . . . Got it off a lad on the train . . In the Merchant Navy . . .

JOYCE. Give him a kiss, man . . .

ERIC. She's changed . . . Hasn't she . . . Look at her . . . *You* used to be the bonny one in the family, didn't you, Joyce . . .

HELEN. Don't be daft, Eric, man . . .

ANDIE. Gone to Birmingham . . Has he . . . Norman? . . .

HELEN. His Mam's upset . . . With Tony missing . . .

ERIC (with banana). You know what to *do* with it, do you, Helen?

HELEN. I'm not as green as I was when we started the war, Eric . . I think so, love . . .

JOYCE. Ee . . . Don't, Helen, man . . .!

ERIC. Are we going to the bonfire, Mrs. Stott?

MAM. Not me . . . I'm not going to any bloody bonfire to show
meself up . . . With all the Fathers watching . . .

GEORGE. Peggy, man . . .

ANDIE. You all right then . . . Helen?

HELEN. I'm cannie . . . Are you?

ANDIE. Never think about it . . . Doesn't matter . . does it? . . .
As good as I'll ever be . . .

ERIC. Come on Mrs. Stott . . . Be a sport . . .

MAM. Not with that bloody communist dummy . . . I am not going . . .

ANDIE. Stick on a label . . 'Lord Haw Haw' and burn that bugger
instead . . .

GEORGE. Five years . . . Bloody fighting for yer freedom . . .

ANDIE. Told ye, didn't I . . . Exactly the same thing in 1918 . . .

HELEN (to AUDIENCE). When we went out into the street . . .
Everything was lit up . . . The whole world was lit . . . There was
something burning really bright in the distance . . . I think it was
the flares on the Eldon statue . . .

MAM. Ee . . The lights . . Look at them, Helen . . Love . . . I can't
get over them . . . Can you . . . Listen . . . There's a late mass . . .
tonight . . Will you come with us, love . . .

HELEN. I might do, Mam . . . I might . . .

(To AUDIENCE:) . . . Too many things had happened to us . . .
that day . . . I was still drained inside us . . . whenever I thought of
Norman . . . It was like a real pain in my body . . . It stabbed us . . .
Every time I thought of him . . .
They all went back into the house . . . I stood on the pavement
taking everything in . . . The whole of Welbeck Road was a string
of lights . . . People making their way to the Park for the
bonfire . . . Eric called out to us . . .

ERIC. Eh Helen, man. Come and dance with us.

HELEN (to AUDIENCE). . . . . I was going to say to him . . .
'Eric . . I can't dance' . . Then I remembered I did . . I *could* . .
now . . . And I let him put his arms round us . . . And dance us
away . . .

HELEN (*to* ERIC). . . Eric . . . I really enjoyed that banana . . .

(*To* AUDIENCE:) I really did, too . . .

They all sing 'Roll Out the Barrel'.

The End

Eyre Methuen also publish

The Master Playwrights

A series of value-for-money paperback play collections by the best modern dramatists

John Arden	**Plays: One** Serjeant Musgrave's Dance, The Workhouse Donkey, Armstrong's Last Goodnight
Brendan Behan	**The Complete Plays** The Hostage, The Quare Fellow, Richard's Cork Leg, Moving Out, A Garden Party, The Big House
Edward Bond	**Plays: One** Saved, Early Morning, The Pope's Wedding **Plays: Two** Lear, The Sea, Narrow Road to the Deep North, Black Mass, Passion
Noël Coward	**Plays: One** Hay Fever, The Vortex, Fallen Angles, Easy Virtue **Plays: Two** Private Lives, Bitter-Sweet, The Marquise, Post-Mortem **Plays: Three** Design for Living, Cavalcade, Conversation Piece, *and* Hands Across the Sea, Still Life *and* Fumed Oak *from* Tonight at 8.30 **Plays: Four** Blithe Spirit, This Happy Breed, Present Laughter, *and* Ways and Means, The Astonished Heart *and* 'Red Peppers' *from* Tonight at 8.30
Henrik Ibsen *Translated and introduced by Michael Meyer*	**Plays: One** Ghosts, The Wild Duck, The Master Builder **Plays: Two** A Doll's House, An Enemy of the People, Hedda Gabler **Plays: Three** Rosmersholm, Little Eyolf, The Lady from the Sea **Plays: Four** John Gabriel Borkman, The Pillars of Society, When We Dead Awaken
Joe Orton	**The Complete Plays** Entertaining Mr. Sloane, Loot, What the Butler Saw, The Ruffian on the Stair, The Erpingham Camp, Funeral Games, The Good and Faithful Servant
Harold Pinter	**Plays: One** The Birthday Party, The Room, The Dumb Waiter, A Slight Ache, A Night Out **Plays: Two** The Caretaker, Night School, The Dwarfs, The Collection, The Lover, five revue sketches **Plays: Three** The Homecoming, Tea Party, The Basement, Landscape, Silence, six revue sketches
Strindberg	**The Father, Miss Julie, The Ghost Sonata** introduced and translated by Michael Meyer